# Bare

## An Unzipped Anthology

edited by
### Valley Haggard & Cindy Cunningham

Issue 6 —— 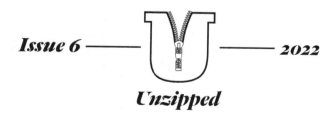 —— 2022

Unzipped

# Bare

**An Unzipped Anthology**

First published in 2022 by
**Life in 10 Minutes Press**
**Richmond, VA**

**lifein10minutes.com/press**

Distributed by IngramSpark
& Life in 10 Minutes Press

ISBN 978-1-949246-17-9

Printed in the United States of America

First Printing, 2022

# About *Life in 10 Minutes*

*Life in 10 Minutes* is a community of writers sharing stories that are brave and true through classes, workshops, retreats, Zoom, and our online lit mag. Visit **lifein10minutes.com** to read deep, strange, hilarious, heartbreaking, and powerful stories written 10 minutes at a time, and share yours, too!

Homegrown in Richmond, Virginia, *Life in 10 Minutes Press* began with the mission to give passage to books we believe in. We seek to bring readers titles that are brave, beautiful, raw, heartfelt, and vital, and to nurture authors in their publishing journeys.

Learn more at **lifein10minutes.com/press.**

*Our mission: We are especially passionate about memoir by women and under-represented voices, nonfiction that challenges the status quo, and boundary-breaking books of all genres. All works published with* Life in 10 Minutes Press *are carefully chosen to support our mission and reflect our commitment to promoting fresh, engaging, high-quality storytelling.*

# About the Cover Art

Annie Ward Love is a self-taught visual artist based in Richmond, Virginia. Mostly large-scale abstract oil paintings, her work is process-oriented and relies on spiritual practice to transcend the limits of the conscious mind. Using mantras such as "Creator creates freely through me," she strives to express all that she does not understand.

*Selves* is an image of connection, longing, homesickness, and mystery. Painted during a period of quarantine at the beginning of the COVID-19 pandemic, it also reflects feelings of isolation, fear of the unknown, the dismantling of illusions, and the loss of a seemingly predictable world. Brushstroke by brushstroke, the painting seemed to create itself. The artist had no plan or vision of a finished product, but believes that the imagery flowed through her from some unknown realm that is within us all, and can be accessed by anyone at any time. The power and magic of the work lies in the unique perspective of each viewer, whose stories and feelings about the image are as valuable and meaningful as those of the artist.

# Welcome to *Unzipped*

*Life in 10 Minutes* fosters love of the immediate. Of the present. The truth. As close up as we can possibly get. *At Life in 10 Minutes,* we reveal life in this moment, right here, right now. Feelings and memories rise from our bodies and spill onto the page. Our stories have curled into knots in our stomachs, fists squeezed around our hearts, pressure against our lungs. We allow these stories to unfurl in our notebooks, releasing us from their grip. As we write, we heal ourselves. As we share our stories, we heal each other. As we heal each other, we heal the world.

Never before has healing the world felt more urgent than now. Now, when connection is more tenuous and precious than ever. When truth is on the chopping block. When the world is on literal and metaphorical fire, when unhealed family and systemic and global trauma threatens to pull us into our most base and destructive selves.

Writing and sharing and reading our stories allows us to process the past, ground in the present and move into the future, freer and more deeply woven into the life-giving, rich fabric of human life. When we write unzipped, we reveal the naked truth, the vulnerable core. When we write unzipped, we join a community of other writers who agree to hold each other's stories and bear witness, to listen, to believe. To create space for the sacred and profane to exist together on the page.

Punctuation is not our first priority. You might find minor errors. You might see a mistake on the page. Sometimes the writing will reflect the chaotic messiness of urgency. We decided that getting the work out there was more important than getting everything perfect.

*Bare: An Unzipped Anthology,* shares the work of writers who allow their truth, their trauma, their pain and struggle, their infinite beauty and whispers of hope, to breathe life on the page. We are honored and excited to share them with you.

With love,
*Dr. Cindy Cunningham and Valley Haggard, Co-Editors*
*Llewellyn Hensley, Graphic Designer*
*Nadia Bukach, Director of Operations*

# Looking for a past (or future) issue of *Unzipped?*

If you missed past issues, they are available for order on the *Unzipped* website (**lifein1ominutes.com/unzipped**).

Issue 1, *Wild Woman: Memoir in Pieces,* by Cindy Cunningham

Issue 2, *She Lives Here,* by Kristina Hamlett

Issue 3, *Unraveled Intimacies,* Paula Gillison, Lisa Loving, Mary Jo McLauglin, Sema Wray,

Issue 4, *Inheritance,* by David Gerson and Stephen McMaster, and

Issue 5, *There's No Accounting for the Strangeness of Things,* by Valley Haggard,

Issue 7 will introduce Sita Romero's micro memoir in which she vacillates between the chilling story of what it's like to grow up with a narcissistic, addict mother and what it's like to deal with aggressive cancer as an adult mother. The language sways from haunting to humorous, from objective to full-on in-the-moment sit-in-it emotion. You will learn the scientific language of -omas, the nonverbal cues between cancer patients, the breaking points between mothers and daughters, and the role of forgiveness in unforgivable situations. Sita's is a memoir you don't want to miss.

— *Life in 10 Minutes Press*

# About Life in 10 Minutes Press

**About the press:**
Homegrown in Richmond, VA, *Life in 10 Minutes Press* seeks to give passage to brave, beautiful, raw, heartfelt, and vital works as we nurture writers in their publishing journey.

Learn more at *lifein10minutes.com/press.*

Mission: We are especially passionate about memoir by women and under-represented voices, nonfiction that challenges the status quo, and boundary-breaking books of all genres. All works published with *Life in 10 Minutes Press* are chosen carefully to support our mission and reflect our commitment to promoting fresh, engaging, high-quality storytelling.

We are infinitely grateful to our patrons who make it possible for us to continue publishing urgent, brave, and true stories. Subscription is the best way to support our mission, and helps us cover the costs associated with producing our quarterly magazine.

To subscribe, visit **www.lifein10minutes.com/unzipped.**

# Contents

### SECTION II — HOW WE SURVIVE

### SECTION III — LETTING GO

# Introduction

We are thrilled to introduce *Bare: An Unzipped Anthology,* a collection of 43 unique pieces by 35 writers — some of whom are long time members of the Life in 10 Minutes community, some of whom are joining us for the first time. Some of our writers have published widely while others are debuting within these pages, but they all have at least one thing in common: they were willing to shed the layers necessary to bare the truth of their pasts, their secrets, and their hearts. Herein they grant us inside views of the body, identity, sexuality, depression, loss, hunger, and mental illness, as well as deep love, gratitude, acceptance and the bittersweet joy of remembering times and people that have passed.

The stories stand on their own, but from the opening sentence of Jer Long's essay, when the bullies say "Let's butt in front of the fat boy" to the closing of the book, when Linda Laino asks, "Was it enough? Your life?" you will find connections and themes so strong that the collection also feels like a community voice making bare its inner landscape of physical pain, emotional pain, moments of self discovery, claiming new identities, and coming through to the other side of loss.

These writers come out of closets, their own skins, and the societies that have layered them with unwanted identities. They write large, they survive, they know how to let go and live a life.

— Dr. Cindy Cunningham & Valley Haggard, Co-Editors

# I

# Written
# Large

# Written Large
## *Jer Long*

"Let's butt in front of the fat boy," the thin track star joked with the trim basketball star as they stepped before me in the cafeteria line my first day of high school. I felt three feet tall and thirty feet wide.

The gay world demanded three things when I busted out of the closet in 1977. To be David Cassidy slim, Tom Selleck mustachioed, and John Travolta disco clad were the basic requirements. Charm and wit, I was warned, was the ticket to the ball, but no one danced with the large lady, even if she sang.

Would I ever get laid?!

"Sorry," I was informed after my audition for *Annie Get Your Gun*. "You're not quite what we're looking for." To translate, "Rotund roustabouts need not apply." I belted better than any of the competition, but the handsome, thin tenor who sang like a braying Billy goat won the prize.

Steering clear of my bulimic mother's example of weight control, I hit the running track the next day. I plunged into the deep end of a dietary obsession that taunted me for the next thirty years. Like

Maria Callas, who strived to look like Audrey Hepburn, I ate only lean meat and salad. Cheese, peanut butter, starchy vegetables, sweets, and Grandma Florence's coconut-butter-cream cake never passed my pouty pink lips.

Victory! I returned to school that fall transformed. Sleek, chic, and magnifique, I was crowned king of my class. I scored the lead in *The Music Man* and escorted the head cheerleader to the prom. Baby, get off my runway. Everything was coming up roses!

I spent the eighties being wined, dined, and courted by the rich, the pretty, the luscious, the winning, the wicked, and the good.

Allowing myself one splurge meal a week, Sunday brunch became an all-I-could-scarf-down. My gorge fest was more disturbingly engrossing than Farrah Fawcett's frosted, feathered fringe.

At 38, I moved in with my partner, a master in the kitchen. Trapped in Hansel & Gretel's edible cottage, my fancy tripped the light fantastic. I would have sold Little Red Riding Hood and her tenderly roasted granny to the wolf for a second helping of ANYTHING! I grew "pleasingly plump."

My metabolism dipped to the speed of Looney Tunes' Cecil Turtle. I worked out harder for less than stellar results. The more I fretted, the more I stuffed my pie-hole. To heighten the horror, my hair fell out with every lick of the brush until my bald father stared back at me from the bathroom mirror.

Over the next twenty years, I tried Squash, Pilates, Acupuncture, Weightlifting, Swimming, and Hot Yoga, which only produced a hot mess. No diet was too extreme. I suffered little success and loads of defeat with Scarsdale's scary weigh-ins, the Mediterranean diet's mad macrobiotics, and Dr. Gundry's perplexing Plant

Paradox Diet. The cabbage diet stirred up tremendous winds down South. The vinegar diet burned a hole in my esophagus. Anxious, angry, and starved, the intoxicating aroma of hot grease lured me into a McDonald's in Miami. I came this close to snatching a darling toddler's Happy Meal® from his grubby grip.

Surrounded by the emaciated, ripped aliens on Miami Beach, I knelt before the vast Atlantic and prayed for the Universe to guide me to the promised land of euphoric skinny.

"What's your weight, sir?" the lady asked as she snapped my new driver's license photo.

"My story's written large," I replied.

An aged, hefty homo is an embarrassing joke that morphs into an invisible commodity in the gay community. I had passed my expiration date. Rejection was stamped on my formidable love-handle. I was no longer admitted to the party.

Two years ago, a friend I hadn't seen in eighteen years announced he would be passing through Richmond. "We must get together," I said, wishing to eat the words that just popped out of my mouth. Why not? I'd eaten everything else.

I struggled to breathe in my Spanx tank top guaranteed to smooth and slenderize the most stubborn bulge. I had to cut my way out!

Motivated by fear, I restricted my caloric intake. Salads, vegetable broth, fizzy water, and panic were my script to success. By the time my friend crossed the Mason-Dixon line, I was three pounds from my ideal weight. Off I trotted to the Jefferson for afternoon tea.

As with Ben Franklin's key dangling from the tail of a kite, the sight of the triple tiered selections of spiritual sweets and salacious savories electrified me. Quivering like a cannabis-laced, sex-starved high school virgin under the bleachers at homecoming, I wrestled my cravings.

Polite nibbling of a petite éclair led to swallowing a lemon custard square whole. With lightning speed, I sawed through a raspberry tart and three-fourths of the finger offerings before my friend finished his sliver of sliced salmon on rye. A tubby toad on holiday, I leapt into the river of deadly delights.

This past September, I had total knee replacement surgery. "Most patients gain fifteen pounds during rehabilitation," my doctor said.

An overachiever, I gained twenty on top of the ten I'd been at war with for the past twelve seasons.

Eight months post-surgery, I, a COVID-19 vaccinated sixty-three-year-old was in a quandary. Thirteen pounds from my ideal weight, I, by the standards of the Fabulous and Fortunate, should've been locked in a tower and hooked to an I.V. of Diet Shasta until I was Timothée Chalamet slim.

Surprisingly, pandemic confinement loosened my drawstring drawers and my attitude. Standing silent on the precipice of a new dawn, I reflected on my years of self-loathing. Others' expectations, I realized, were a crime against my nature. I raised my middle finger to judgmental swine and selected MODERATION as my future weapon of choice.

Slow and steady could win the race. With proper portions, I may enjoy my cake and eat it too. Fingers crossed!

# Queer
## *Joan Mazza*

Since the anniversary of Stonewall, I've been thinking about queer, how the word has been an insult and accusation, a taunt meant to hurt and exclude, unless the word refers to oneself. Now it rings with confidence and bravery. Defiance, too.

Am I queer? Depends on who you ask. What I usually share of my life seems ordinary enough: a woman born female and female identified, married young to a man. Once. Divorced. No children.

Have I not at times been queer?

Dissatisfied with monogamy, I sought novelty, curious about paraphilias. B&D, S&M, rubber and latex didn't appeal to me. My preference for groups wasn't listed. Orientation or a passing kink?

Briefly, I thought of myself as bi because I was attracted to women as well as men. Preferably both together, but my experience was limited and complicated by others' power. I wanted a threesome with a woman. My male lover wanted a threesome with another man, expected he'd be director. Maybe neither of us could admit our real desires. Perhaps we needed an intermediary—an ooloi, to give us permission.

Then I saw myself as polyamorous, preferred honest, consensual non-monogamy rather than betrayal by cheaters. How much better to know the deal, have it transparent and clear. But make a rule such as, no one other than the two of us in our bed, and that becomes forbidden fruit, more taste than the bowl with variety outside our door.

Who isn't queer?

If I understood—no, grokked—some choices, such as celibacy or a desire to be career military, I might have made those selections, too, and not thought of them as strange or perverse. Queer.

June day in a public park, I look around. The bare-chested male who is pierced and tattooed on every inch of skin that shows, including one side of his face. Is he queer? If that were a woman, would those decorations be more than queer?

We say someone has a fetish for rubber, leather, or lace, but what about a collection of animal bones and skulls? Or taxidermied wolves and foxes instead of crystal candy dishes? Is it a fetish only if it's sexually arousing for the owner? How about shotguns and swords on the walls, an abhorrence for paintings, photographs, and macramé?

I've had enough of human connection and its friction. Pandemic isolation has been a luxury, a gift. Now I love solitude and silence, revel in autonomy.

Call me a sexual outlaw. Call me queer.

# Behold: a fairy is born!
*erin gerety*

Burst forth from the womb, cradled by Penguin Cafe Orchestra, swaddled in blankets of Captain Beefheart and The Beach Boys. From bare feet on the earth of a Nebraska trailer park, from the train tracks of Falls City where my blood mother was born to run to the arms of a Connecticut record store clerk who loved her long blonde hair and her cornfed ass and the slow way she sifted through a rack of cassettes. Together they brought this world one more fae raised on salted radishes and strawberries, Jacko Pastorious, Stevie Nicks, and Kate Bush.

But all was not as it seemed, b/w, there's always darkness hiding near the light, and of course the fairy was trapped for years in a lantern ten sizes too small, fed pages from hymnals, laminated pages of praise & worship songs, processed foods and blood red meat from a family of cattle kings and army men.

Tiny moments of solace found in a pair of headphones pouring spells from only what the fairy knew how to feed themselves: morsels of Michelle Branch and Bjork, gulps of Hole and Avril Lavigne, a sip of Destiny's Child...

Eventually they saw themselves stuck in a cage still while their light grew brighter and brighter, far too bright to be held in such a minuscule lantern. So the fairy fled to a town where the streets pulsed with synthwave and d-beat, braided their hair with seapunk and dreampop, found themselves finally alight and alive.

Splitting a pair of stolen headphones across the center console, screaming words out of a car window with the cold winter air twisting back through smoke through hair. In the back of a basement as the crowd swells with sweat and beer. Feet forward on the kitchen floor eating as much fresh fruit as their flesh can hold.

# Love Letter to Venus
## *Kali Fillhart*

My mom used to ask me why I dressed like a boy. I didn't have an answer. Somehow my body already knew that being a girl meant pain, labor, rejection. Maybe if I disguised myself I won't have to bear the weight of lineage on my shoulders. The women in my family complain about hips, breasts, and periods and I want nothing to do with them.

\*\*\*

My dad's father dies when I'm 14, but it's my mother who decides church is the answer to whatever guilt she won't talk about. We never went to church before. My mom's side is the godless type and somewhere this may be in me because I am not willing to go. I cry and yell and make sure the world knows that I'm not the kind of person who believes in just anything. I am the reasonable one. Logical. Correct. My mother's the lost soul grasping for straws. Not me at 14 and grieving.

\*\*\*

In high school, I starve. I am distant. Ignored. English homework, swim team, band practice, family dinner. 4 a.m. alarm clocks, math test on Thursday, weekend shifts at the downtown Subway. Hit the gym in the morning. Stare at body in the mirror for thirty minutes. Weigh before shower. Protein bars for breakfast, lunch, and dinner. I imagine my grandmother weighing herself in 1930s Poland. How ridiculous it would have been. With the children and the food and the cleaning and grandpa not coming home again. How would her mother have responded to wrist slits and melancholy? Maybe it is her starved soul I feel in my clavicle and hip bones. I can see her rib cage in mine, my mother's eyes now mine, their hands covering my mouth, their words and sorrows. We survived. So will you.

***

In college, I shatter. I am a sleepless, carpal-tunnel ridden, starved headache of a human. Friendships lost for being a slut. Friendships lost for not being a slut. Mom asks why I can't visit home more often. Claims home is the two story they moved into a month before I left for college. When I visit I sleep on a pull out couch. The dog hair makes me wheeze. I try to explain complex rational equations, Shang dynasty literature, the Cambodian genocide of the 1970s, and how to say, "No thank you, I am sick," in Russian. She tells me to be grateful and we don't talk for a couple of weeks.

***

A runaway summer road trip to LA turns into a gap year in Portland, Oregon. I tell my professors it's for research, participant observation, a thought experiment for learning purposes only, but we can all see through time and wonder if I'll ever come back. I've never been to the West Coast before. I've never looked at the stars but an astrology school in the northeast part of town, a home of sorts for the questionable, speaks to the wanderers in my bloodstream. I am an East Coast runaway with starved roots, desperate and motherless. I enroll in the first year program and wait.

***

And when I tell you I shook, day one, my body shook. I realize I never wanted answers, not the ones my mother needed. I wanted questions. The right questions. The monsoon of a Mars and Neptune conjunction, north node in Virgo, Mercurial on the ascendent aspected Chiron's open wound. Piscean oceans, Capricorn enclaves surrounded by a Sagittarius wildfire bucking itself clean. Star talking peers with the same craving, the same addiction to asking. We talk for hours on the nuances of chart signatures and astrological ethics. We act out scenes of our most intense natal aspects. My Sagittarius sun and Gemini moon opposition are on stage, screaming at each other. Why don't you know more, asks the Gemini moon. Why can't you learn deeper, begs the Sagittarius Sun. Why aren't you better, why can't you stay still, why are you always thinking, why are you always gone, why can't you take care of us, why, why, why, why.

\*\*\*

My altar is an altar of action. On the fireplace in the bedroom I rent. As any good mystic will tell you, there is no magic without action. Nor is there magic without rest and contemplation. Venus and Mars. The home and the bulldozer. I have a candle burning for Aquarius energy, a candle for good fortune, and a candle for my ancestors. I have crystals- rose quartz, selenite, rhodonite, smoky quartz. Vitamins, sugar cookies, and kombucha. Red lipstick bought from Cheek-Bone beauty, an indigenous owned, ethically made makeup brand. The tinctures for grounding, the CBD bag and pipe for calming, the golden dollar bill for attracting, and the hot pink lighter for burning.

A couple weeks ago I bought an electric drum kit, a middle-tier brand, black pads with red detail. On good days, I learn new songs, advance songs outside my skill range. On harder days, I play *Seven Nation Army* and *I Love Rock and Roll* over and over again until my kick pedal calf is throbbing and the ching of the high hat rattles my teeth. This is my body's way of expressing gratitude for existing. I like to think I come from musicians somewhere down the line and this is my way of saying *hello, nice to be with you today.* Maggie, my hairless, questionable breed of a 7-pound rescue dog, sleeps in my arms. I rub her skin with coconut oil and massage her paws, nurturing her wounds as she leans her fragile head against my shoulder. Men have gone to war to meet God. I take a simpler route and find her here, in the quiet vibrations of the body, the home, in a full stomach and easy breathing. Always something to heal. Always something to become.

# The Bug Years
## *Lee Sowder*

The '63 Volkswagen was my third bug. The first one was a '68 and powder blue, the one I bought from Ernie when I came back from Austin, the one my mother bought me for going back to college. It made it through graduation and another trip to Austin, then died on Riverside Drive in South Austin days before my grandmother died and my mother wired me airfare to fly back to Virginia. The second bug was a red '65 that Ernie sold for parts after I flipped it into Back Creek at the bottom of Bent Mountain after a night of drinking tequila and smoking pot. The smell of rust and blood forever intertwined in my memory of Volkswagen smells and scents, to this day.

That '63 took me down to the Florida Keys for a winter. I was twenty-five. I took the back seat out and made a bed from down comforters and pillows and lined it with my clothes and coolers along the floor, covering up the one rusted out spot that saw daylight and let in fumes when the bug was starting up.

I had quit my job working at a facility for emotionally disturbed adolescents, the one where the teen from Philadelphia had cornered me in the bathroom with a broken lightbulb and threatened to cut my face, the one that punished the teen by upping her meds and moving her to isolation for a week. The one I swore I would never work at again.

I was giving up my apartment, leaving Roanoke right after Christmas with my six-month-old puppy Joe Bear, a mix between a German Shepherd and a wolf, and my two-year-old white cat Sugar. My mother was a single mother. My father had died when I was eight, and as independent as she was, she could not hold back her worry that I was putting myself, a single young woman, in grave danger by traveling alone.

"Lee, that car of yours might not even make it to South Carolina. You could be stranded on the road. I pray the good Lord keeps you safe, but you are putting yourself in danger."

I promised to call her every Saturday morning.

My mother never believed that I would be safe, not until I traveled back to Virginia all those months later, but I did call her every Saturday, from pay phones in Key West and Sugarland Key and New Orleans and Austin, and all the other places in between. It was time for me to run from myself and toward myself, to leave and to become. I crossed the seven-mile bridge on a clear windless day with Joe Bear leaning out the back window and Sugar curled around my neck watching the water turn blue and green and silver, light tinting our views and salt air as soothing as a lullaby.

Daytime in Key West is overrated. Most people are sleeping off hangovers or swimming in the corals or out on a boat somewhere. It was not the ideal time to pull into town for the very first time, with no idea on where to go or what to do. Key West had been my destination dream and I had no ideas on what that meant. I only knew I was leaving a life that confused and scared me, one I was ready to turn out with the trash. I didn't know yet who the new me would be, only that I didn't like the old me. The years it would take to discover that so much of that fear and loathing had to do with my sexuality and my resistance to accepting who I was, a lesbian, instead of the straight marriage version of myself I had assumed, were not wasted time. But I was lost. And driving to Key West would be my first step to finding my way back, to me.

I pulled into Leo's campground around 4pm and paid the ten dollars for one night. The campground was expensive and basically a concrete parking lot with a bathhouse. The temperature was in the eighties even though it was early January and the black faux leather front seats were hot to the touch. Sugar curled up under the bug, the only shade inside, and Joe Bear walked with me down the alleyways of Key West, looking for shade and spots to pee. I had heard about sunsets in Key West, and as I made my way towards the docks, I felt a stirring excitement, mingling with a nervous fear of the unknown. The numbness I had kept myself in through drugs and alcohol was wearing down. For the first time, I began feeling a power belonging to me, a power saying I am in charge, I am in charge of my life and I am making it good.

Sloppy Joe's was on the way to the docks, and even though Joe Bear wasn't allowed inside, a waitress was nice enough to take my order and my money and bring out a beer and hamburger to the door. While I was thanking her, I asked if she knew of any campgrounds to stay in.

"Oh, Leo's is a rip off. Go down to the KOA two keys down on Sugarland Key. It's only five dollars a day and has big fields to camp in. You'll be fine cutie." She winked at me then and walked back inside.

As much as I wanted to go right then and find the KOA, I was too tired, and I had already spent the ten dollars on the night. Money was not going to last a whole winter, I would need a job, and even ten dollars spent needed to be used up the way it was intended. I walked on over to the docks and found a park bench, Joe Bear lying at my feet, looking out over the water and the slew of tourists and hippies and musicians filing in, setting up for sunset.

# Who We Might Become
## *Patricia Smith*

Years ago, reading Lucy Calkins' book on teaching writing, I was struck by an interview with the children's author, Avi. When he was asked for advice for how to teach children to write, he said, "First you have to love them. Then you can teach them anything." I was a young teacher when I read those words, and I tried to take them to heart. We teachers love so many children, and they don't always know that what we are doing is love, that our chiding and our pushing and even sometimes our complaining, is love, perhaps the deepest kind of love.

Sometimes, loving our students is hard -- trying to explain to 7th- grade boys why a "babe-o-meter" isn't a cool invention during our 7th grade activity period, or to the girls why being rated highly isn't exactly as great as they think. Or watching them tease and exclude, helping them in their greatest distress to become just who they are supposed to be.

That is, after all, our job. To help our students become who they are supposed to be, in all their complications.

Recently, I had a rare opportunity to meet up with a former student. It is years after I have taught Stephanie. She's married now, and she and her wife are also both teachers, spending their summers in Provincetown. One summer, we reconnect there. We're at brunch, getting caught up on all the intervening years between 7th grade and now. Stephanie was, I remember, a student who was easy to love—gregarious and funny. I might have called her a spitfire. Now, in the summer sunshine, the patio full of Provincetown regulars and tourists, Stephanie takes a deep breath. "I have to say this," she says. "It has been on my mind for years."

She launches into a story. "Remember when..." and she sends us back to that earlier lifetime, me, walking with a group of 12 -and 13-year-olds, all of us participating in the annual Walk for Hunger, a 20-mile fundraiser for Project Bread in Massachusetts. We're near the end and the kids are straggling and Stephanie tells a gay joke. "And then," present-day Stephanie recounts, "you just kind of smiled. You didn't yell at me or make me feel like a jerk. You said, 'you know, Stephanie. Your mind is like a parachute. It only works when it's open' and you just kept on walking."

I laugh now because it was exactly the kind of thing I would've said to my 7th graders, those gangly kids I used to teach, spilling into my classroom every fall, all of them on the verge of becoming who they might be, and me, in my twenties, thinking I was going to show them the world and teach them how to speak French, but really what I was -- what we all are-- teaching them is how to be.

"I have to apologize," Stephanie says. "For years, I've been a little horrified that I told that joke and I always remember how you handled it."

We hug and laugh together on this Provincetown Sunday, the irony of her gay joke not lost on either of us, she with her wife and me with mine. But inside, I am also nervously thankful that I didn't humiliate her back then; I so easily could have. I am grateful for the grace that showed up in that moment, that allowed us to all keep walking, the kids dragging their blistered feet those last miles to the finish line on Boston Common.

It would have been May and already warm. We would have been nearing the end of our school year together. The 8th graders in our group would have been getting ready to leave our school and head off to high school. We all would have just spent an entire year together, conjugating verbs, learning to ask questions, talking about ourselves and our families, perhaps even moving from past tense to present and future.

# I Just Wanted to Dance
## *Donna Joyce*

I dropped off my 16-year-old daughter at the mall to see her friends, socially-distanced. We are one year into the pandemic, April 2021, and life still feels unsafe but better than it did throughout all of 2020. I drove back home in the car that has Sirius radio, listening to the U2 Channel, and caught a segment I had heard advertised called "Adam Clayton's Disco Playlist." Adam Clayton is the bassist for the four man post-punk rock band from Ireland called U2.

The idea that U2 would have a disco playlist just blew my mind in the best possible way because I love, I mean I LOVE disco. I love the music, the lyrics, the glitz, AND I love to DANCE! And disco was often impossible to find on the radio after the disco vs. rock wars of 1979, which was, unbeknownst to me at the time, promoted through racism and sexism in the music industry, causing real riots in Chicago and LA. I just saw it in the form of kids yelling at each other at a junior high school dance, "Disco Sucks, Rock Rules!" and "Rock Sucks, Disco Rules!" I was definitely on the losing side with disco. I didn't hate rock, I just loved to dance so disco was so much more fun for me. I eventually was able to replace rock that again took over the radio with late punk, early new wave by standing very still in one spot in my sister's bedroom, near the old portable record player on the floor. That was the only way we could listen to WLIR 92.7FM, a radio station broadcast out of Port Washington which was many miles away in the next county on Long Island, New York. It did not have its frequency broadcast from the top of the Empire State Building like other radio stations. It was broadcast from a fairly tall building in the suburbs and it was totally worth figuring out where to stand in the house in order to hear it. My sister's bedroom was the only room we were able to get it tuned in. She set her boombox up, both of us standing near the record player and doing whatever kind of dancing we could, basically wiggling in place, to the B-52s, Duran Duran, Adam Ant, Joan Jett. It was also where I first heard U2 sing and play and speak straight to my heart. They were my band. I truly do not know how I would have gotten through high school and my family's divorce without them.

About a month into the pandemic, I started driving around my city, Richmond, VA, after I got tired of not going out anymore. At first it had been so delicious not to drive anywhere, or rather, not to have to drive anywhere. I did not have to drop off nor pick up anyone. I didn't have to drive to anything. I loved it because I hate driving, at least I hate suburban driving. I really miss reliable extensive NYC mass transit — which I hear is no longer reliable. Too bad. Public transit is a beautiful thing. But a secret treasure during the pandemic became driving around to different neighborhoods with my windows down blasting my favorite music, especially disco from the Sirius radio Studio 54 Channel. It felt fun!

My 16 year old makes fun of me for loving disco, but she also likes it, probably because I played it so much for my kids when they were little. They know it makes people happy.

Driving around listening to U2's Adam Clayton talk about the history of disco evolving from funk felt so perfect — he's a bassist and funk is rooted in the bass line. I found myself thinking about an idea I have considered before, but it seems like it would be useful during the pandemic, turning my car or a van or a truck into a disco mobile and just hanging out on a corner in a neighborhood, DJing — my initials are DJ! — for folks to come out onto the street and dance for a little during the day. I think this idea springs from hanging out in Central Park on Sunday afternoons and seeing the disco roller skaters come and bring their boombox and sound system equipment to get some volume, a sound boundary for the kind of roller disco they recreated each weekend near the bandshell. So happy, so fun, and sometimes a fist fight, broken up by fellow skaters. They all seemed to know each other. I loved to watch.

I'm trying to remember what age I was when I first went to a disco. I know I was in junior high, maybe 1977 or 78. I think *Saturday Night Fever* had come out that year and the BeeGees were super popular. I know I was "underage" — the disco, called '2001', was in the Marshall's Shopping Center, one town over from mine and it opened during the day for teenagers. I might have been 11 or 12 and I think I needed to be 13 in order to get in so I had to lie about what year I was born. They didn't check ID's because we didn't have any, but they would just ask what year you were born. I went with my friends Jean and Michelle. Michelle was the one who told us that we needed to lie and how to do it, because she had an older brother who knew about the disco even though he played drums in a rock band. Michelle, Jean and I had been friends for most of elementary school, all through Girl Scouts and would ride our bikes around neighboring towns every weekend. We went to the roller rink and the movies, putt putt golf, together. So many sleepovers. But this was something different. It was something that felt more adult, and

I was excited about it. I was also a little scared because the second time we went, an older man tried to hit on Michelle. We all were grossed out and couldn't believe it had happened. Was it because we had lied about our age? Why would that man hit on a teenager anyway? So many questions for the future. Michelle ran out. Jean and I did too. We never went back. Our parents were against us going in the first place so we never said anything about the creepy old guy. But I really wanted to go somewhere to dance. One of the times that we went, we saw a boy who was a couple of years older than us, Mike D. He was on the raised dance floor that flashed red, green, blue and yellow lights like the one in *Saturday Night Fever*. My very favorite disco song "Knock On Wood" by Amii Stewart started playing and he was dancing to it, alone, like the people who ran the disco already knew who he was and that this was his solo. I don't know about Michelle and Jean but I was transfixed. I had never seen a guy I knew dance so well — he definitely put John Travolta to shame. I felt like this was a special treat for me, this being my favorite song and all. I also felt like I was witnessing a secret life of Mike D at the 2001 disco.

Two years later, '2002', the roller disco opened up. It was a more welcoming space for a teenager. But I didn't really want to skate. I wanted to dance.

# Origin Story
## *Priscilla Cash*

My childhood was written entirely in the Shenandoah Valley of Virginia, surrounded by gentle mountain ranges and acres and acres of fields and farmlands. It has been a place of agricultural plenty for centuries. We lived there as a non-farming family after my father took a starter job repossessing cars for a local bank. His new banking gig paid the bills, *almost*. Both my father and my mother were extremely hard workers. But as young parents, they struggled to keep all of us in clothes, shoes, and food.

For part of my childhood, my family was *food insecure,* a sanitized label that I've always felt completely missed the mark. Our situation was no one's fault. My parents did their best with their high school diplomas. But sometimes there just wasn't enough. This wounded my father in particular. And I can still see that reflected in his soft brown eyes.

If my mother's spirit ever struggled under the weight of nine mouths to feed, I never knew it. She was smiley and playful. And made a childhood adventure out of *foraging* for food, piloting us each week to local farms along rural Route 11, by pastures of grazing Holstein cows, corn fields, and squat barracks of chicken houses that scented the valley with their fecund aromas. To this day, I can tell if a field has been fertilized with chicken or cow manure just by rolling down the car windows.

At Bingham's dairy farm, with the car still rolling to a stop, we'd fling open the doors and cut through the flowering mustard and Indian tobacco in our race to see the newborns. They would wobble toward us, trailed by their hoof-thudding mothers. Carefully negotiating the wide gaps in the electric fence, I would strain to be nose to nose with the calves, drinking in their breath, sweetened with early spring grasses and mother's milk. We would always leave with a three-gallon glass jar of milk. This was not the early days of the concierge-priced "farm share." This was a gesture of gratitude for a tractor loan my father had helped the man secure. And was our only dairy for the week, whose skimmed cream we would shake in an old canning jar until it *clunked* into a mass of sweet butter.

Our summer was snippets of TV soap operas, singing into box fans, or cooling off under the sprinkler in my mother's backyard garden. Her garden was not a hobby. It was a lifeline. And none of her harvest ever went to waste. Even the rinds of watermelons were somehow delicious after pickling. When we had eaten through the corn, tomatoes, and other vegetables that she had carefully "put up" for the winter, we had skillets of brown beans and cornbread. While I've always credited my father with our safe passage out of poverty, it was my mother who kept us alive along the way.

She made meals from seemingly nothing. A handful of leftover beef, a crushed bouillon cube, flour and milk could be transformed into a thin gravy and spooned over bread, feeding us for lunch. And I regularly saw her wordlessly pass her plate to my father or one of her children when she feared they might not have enough. That's not what *food insecurity* looks like. That is what being hungry and poor looks like.

Yet we were more fortunate than many we knew. We had food assistance. And it came from growers who would drop a bushel of fall apples at our door, a country ham at Christmas, or homemade cracklins from an early November hog slaughter. This sort of informal support was possible in rural America in the 1960s, a time before we began living so shallowly in places. And it sustained us.

The poorest periods of my childhood imprinted a lasting identity I've never wanted to inhabit. Even as a small child, I knew that words like *white trash, lazy, irresponsible* were slung at families like mine. But I couldn't reconcile those labels with the family I knew and loved. We simply were not those things.

Shame about my upbringing was my companion well into adulthood, peaking when I married into a waspy New England family with multigenerational mega wealth. In my husband's social echelon, I pushed my origin story even further underground. I furtively scrubbed off the red clay dust from my selfhood, along with my Southern accent, and watched the last powdery traces of me circle the drain. I felt this necessary to fit in among the country club set with its paradoxically starving society skeletons whose affluence could be measured by the tininess of their Chanel suits.

My husband's childhood dining experiences couldn't have been more different from mine. His family had a live-in cook who laid their dining table with linen, bone china, and sterling silver every evening. She signaled them to the table with a small, silver bell when it was time to settle into their mahogany dining chairs, the ones his parents received as wedding gifts from the Guggenheims. My mother-in-law could be critical of my unrefined palate and often seized on the family dinner as an opportunity to remind me that had I been a New York debutante, like she was, I would be more appreciative of the exotic foods I found before me.

This morning at my kitchen counter I measure a tablespoon of peanut butter to spread on half a banana. I thumb-tap this into my phone which is monitoring my eating. I am rationing food. Not out of scarcity. Out of abundance. I am ashamed.

Early midlife has arrived like a series of killing frosts, blanketing the garden in disease and divorce and despair. I survey the dying landscape, tallying the losses in the frozen leaves and blackened flower heads that still cling to the plants, as if waiting for resurrection. I am gleaning, harvesting what survives of my complex identify. Dead are the shallow, showy cultivars of my marriage-begotten affluence. I pull from the soil what is rooted most deeply. Reflections of my childhood home, the sighing vowels of my mother's voice, the hand-me-downs, and the discomfort of going to bed hungry. It is in these remains that I can regard with great tenderness the young girl turned adult woman who is willing to get close to the homeless person on the corner, to look them in the eye, and to offer them food. Or who bothers to ask them if they know where to find the nearest shelter and a meal. And who makes sure to compliment them on something, anything, like their warm smile, the neat lettering on their cardboard sign, or the artistic rendering of a dog they once loved and now carry with them as a sketch in a tattered spiral notebook. These people are my people. I am them and they are me, separated only by a few degrees of luck or sobriety or mental health, but connected through the gnawing pain of our human relatedness. We are sacred human beings. Sacred beyond the circumstances of our lives. I want them to know my origin story. And I want to know theirs.

# The Eyes of Mercy
## *Andrew Taylor-Troutman*

*What the eye does not see, will not move the heart.*
— Haitian proverb

*Happy are the merciful, for they will receive mercy.*
— Matthew 5:7

My grandmother died in the spring before the coronavirus pandemic; Gran was spared the loneliness and stress of the yearlong lockdown in her assisted living facility. As my former campus minister said, her death was a mercy.

During what turned out to be our last visit, a nurse with a kind smile served each of us a dish of banana pudding. Gran took a spoonful and closed her eyes as she swallowed. Then, her eyes flew open like two birds startled from a tree: "Mercy, that's good!"

Gran was a lifelong Baptist. In the Bible, an act of mercy can also refer to alms-giving. As I slipped a $10 bill into the cracked, red Solo® cup held by a man slumped against a park bench, I remembered my Gran, a stranger's purse, and a morning almost twenty years ago.

The night before, I'd blown all my money at the bar and my last conscious memory was puking in the parking lot. When I awoke with a mind-numbing headache, I did not know where I was, but knew I desperately needed to find my car. The rest of my family expected me at Gran's house for her 70th birthday party. On my way out of the apartment, I pilfered a $10 bill from the purse hung carefully by the back door. Eventually, I found out the identity of the Good Samaritan who'd taken me in for the night, but I denied stealing cigarette money from her.

When I was a boy, I played a cruel game in which adversaries faced off and grasped hands. The point was to bend your opponent's wrists backwards until he dropped to his knees and begged for mercy. It would be another year after Gran's party before I would confess my drug habit and seek help from a campus minister with a great, tangled nest of a beard and tiny hands that zipped like humming-birds when he spoke of unconditional love. He told me that an ancient man named Saint Basil the Great once claimed, "Through mercy to your neighbor, you resemble God."

Saints and priests, shamans and charlatans as well as many addicts can slap $10 words on the ineffable. A scripture, proverb, or well-turned phrase may stick in the mind. But a picture of God is not God; a painting of the ocean does not churn with salt water. At best, a word like "mercy" can only gesture to a sparkle on the face of the deep or Gran's ancient, glittering eyes. Life itself is priceless — a sudden ray of sun breaks through a cloud to angle upon the man holding a red Solo® cup as he catches my eyes and smiles.

# Red Bud
## *Gail Giewont*

When the boys next door received tree saplings at school, they brought them to my house to plant. I explained that my husband did not love the trees that already ringed our house. They insisted. They had nowhere to plant them. (This claim was demonstrably untrue.)

We dug two holes in the backyard, added good soil, and filled buckets with water that we poured over the trees.

When I knew they wouldn't notice, I pulled out the oak sapling by the roots and threw it in the woods. My husband feared the oaks' height, worried every time another strong storm blew through that the existing trees would fall on our house. We let the red bud grow. When the boys asked, I said I didn't know what had happened to the oak tree.

Back then, the boys visited often—to play with the dogs, to help in the garden, to beg for sweets, to check on the status of their red bud. One day, when they were eight years old, they caught me transplanting ornamental grass seedlings into the front garden bed and offered to help. I handed them trowels, explained that the grass was delicate. I had grown the seedlings myself over the past month.

Lucas gave me a seedling to put in the ground.

"Did your baby die?" he asked.

Lucas had been excited when we had told him I was pregnant two years earlier, before Aaron and his mother had come to live next door. He had hoped we would take him to Toys 'R Us with the baby. I had thought he would have forgotten.

I nodded. My lip didn't tremble. I didn't cry—not then. "He was very sick," I said. This was true, if not the whole truth. I pushed dirt around the roots of the grass, and the three of us kept planting, not knowing none of the seedlings would survive.

The boys don't come to check on the red bud now. Aaron doesn't live next door anymore, and Lucas sees his father only sometimes. But each spring, the tree's limbs burst into pink blossoms. Every year, it grows.

# Searching for Penance
## *James Stoneking*

We called him The Wolfman though my boss called him "Wolfie." I never knew his real name. I worked in a pharmacy while in college and there were many interesting customers over the years but The Wolfman was the most memorable. Obviously he wasn't a real were-wolf, wasn't afflicted with lycanthropy, but he fit the bill. He was in his late 80s, short and stocky, a little over five feet tall and walked with a rolling gait from, we assumed, a hip injury. His gaunt skin drooped from his body and was covered in liver spots and wrinkles. His teeth were gnarled and when he shouted at you, which was constant because he couldn't hear, you found yourself assaulted by spittle and rancid breath. His gray hair was an unruly mane, slightly balding on top. The ears, though, were very prominent. They didn't stick out that far but, instead, were extraordinarily long. Not in an elegant elfish way, but thick and hairy with tufts of fur growing out from the inside, competing against his hearing aids. Usually, much like himself, his baggy clothes were dirty, shirts stained from food, pants often threadbare reeking of urine and feces. Brown wing-tips shoes worn and unpolished. His foul appearance was equally matched with his personality; often loud, angry, bitter and verbally abusive to everyone at the pharmacy.

He had a sister who was quite normal, slightly younger. When he spoke about her he would soften his face and actually smile and his eyes would brighten. She rarely accompanied him to the pharmacy, I had only met her once or twice, but she had a calming effect on him. She had also been apologetic about him when we spoke. I knew she didn't live with him but I could tell when she had recently visited the Wolfman. His clothes would be clean, as was he, and his hair was managed. His personality was still offensive for the most part but at least the odor wasn't.

He would come in about twice a month, sometimes for a prescription or other sundries but usually for hearing-aid batteries. There was also something else. He was nearly blind. He could navigate fairly well, but to read, he had to have it inches from his face. You would often hear him yelling for assistance from somewhere in the store to get a price on something only to have him yell to the world, and into your face, how expensive the item was. Eventually my manager decided it was easier to assign a staff member to help him shop in order to cut down on the noise and to get "Wolfie" out of the store faster. I was the chosen one. My boss jokingly told me that it was because I liked antiques, but truthfully neither of us wanted to admit that deep down I was a compassionate person. I cringed every time he came to the store. I didn't hate him but the hygiene made me loathe his existence. It didn't matter where I was or what I was doing, even if I was on my break; I would be called over the intercom to help him. More often than not, I'd catch the sadistic grins from my fellow coworkers as I headed to The Wolfman, resigned to my fate. This went on for nearly three years.

The low point of this arrangement occurred sometime after the second year. While he was yelling at me about the price increase on batteries, he lost control of his bowels and he wasn't wearing a diaper as usual. It was a surreal experience being yelled at while standing in piss and watery shit. Even though this cut his visit short, I wasn't off the hook since I was the one who had to clean the foul, putrid mess. Shortly after that experience he started showing up dressed better and somewhat cleaner. He eventually told me that his sister, his 'beautiful sister', had moved in with him. I never encouraged him to stay any longer than necessary so I didn't ask why she moved in. I was just glad that he wasn't as abusive. About four months later he came in dressed nicer than usual but instead of calling my name like normal, he began sobbing and wailing that his sister had died (he had just left the funeral and was on the way home). I did go over to him and he embraced me, which was shocking, but as he sobbed into my chest I could only think about the hair sticking out of his ears and the slight smell of stale urine. In that moment I had never been so revolted and embarrassed, not with him but with myself.

For the next few months he was in rare form. If anything, he was worse than before in hygiene and attitude. One afternoon I was in the office and heard him come in. I sat there and closed my eyes, trying to wish him away. That week I was writing two papers and studying for exams and was only getting about four hours of sleep and to top it off there were also problems at home. At that moment I just couldn't take The Wolfman. I didn't think I could be civil, I thought that I'd snap and get myself fired. So I just sat there, doing my best to ignore him and his incessant yelling. I remember one of the pharmacy techs coming over, asking if I was alright. I never looked up at her and could only shake my head 'no.' Eventually the pharmacist explained that I wasn't there and offered up another associate to help but The Wolfman refused. Almost whimpering, he said that he'd be back tomorrow. That didn't happen.

It was nearly a month later when the store manager heard that The Wolfman had died several days after his last visit to the store where, thinking only of myself, I had essentially turned him away. He suffered a heart attack while sleeping alone in his house. I felt relief for him. The little bit of his life I saw was one of anger and misery with the only bright spot, his sister, also leaving him (like me) before the end.

# How Am I Doing?
## *Hollee Freeman*

A lot of people have been asking me the ubiquitous question: "So, how are you doing?"

My response is always — "I'm exhausted." Because, well, I actually am exhausted. But perhaps the better thing to say, the truer thing to say would be that I am not well. My elders are not well. Maybe I should let you know that even though I am experiencing the ultimate gift of supporting my elders during their concurrent medical crises, that oftentimes I am moving between not knowing and not knowing.

It might be good if I told you that I don't know how to do this, and I don't even know how to feel. Maybe the really soul-searing thing to tell you is that I don't know what the future holds for me or my elders, and I'm scared and sad about that.

But since you have asked, I have decided to dig deeper and explore how I am doing and how I am doing it.

Well, friend, how I am doing feels like I'm in the water looking at a beautiful beach. The scene only lasts for a moment as huge waves repeatedly and violently knock me down. Waves of sadness, confusion, anger, responsibility, and gratefulness. These powerful waves want me to get up-I know it and I do. I get up.

Sometimes, I look at the wave head-on and brace for it, calling out its name, calling out names of ancestors in reverence and declaring myself strong. But sometimes, I give up for a moment, and try to move back toward the safety of the beach. For this, I get pummeled from the rear, unaware. Unknowing.

Between waves, I see friends and strangers on boats heading toward some serene, fun, expansive place. I am delighted for them. I remember fondly when I enjoyed being on boats, speeding toward some destination. Career boats. Social media boats. Dancing boats. Going out with friends boats.

But for now, I am in the water just trying to remain standing. I am one with the water. I am learning lessons from the water. Lessons of power, faith, perseverance, and love. I don't know what life is like for the people on boats speeding toward their destination. Are they equipped in their very marrow? Can they save their own lives? Are they headed in the right direction? Do they have enough fuel? Are they paying attention?

What I do know is that at this point on this beach in this water, my job is to be flexible and stay erect. To be strong and yield into the water. The water of my ancestors. The water of my elders. That is my only responsibility.

That is how I am doing. Thank you for asking.

# Making Friends with Depression
## *Stella Graham-Landau*

Depression.

I was an early user of Prozac and St. John's Wort and, before that, alcohol. Wanting to feel lighter. Wanting fear and anxiety to lift. Wanting to want to live.

It was a tough time. A relationship would end. A relationship that I thought was fixable. If only we both leaned in. If only we both trusted. If only we both would try. But they weren't destined to continue. They crashed. They burned. They were relationships between addicts and damaged people. And, even after sobriety, they were still relationships reeling in muck.

Why can't you? Why didn't you? Why won't you? Don't you care? Can't you change?

Yet here I am in a relationship almost 33 years long, possible because those other relationships ended. Possible because we both learned about ourselves and each other. Possible because we did lean in and stayed and trusted that the process of rigorous honesty and commitment to growth would prevail.

Depression still visits, but I recognize her. I wave. I offer her a cup of coffee or tea when I see her sitting on the bench, somewhat disheveled, bordered by her bags of possessions which she drags around with her. She manages to smile back at me. Tips her invisible hat to thank me for acknowledging her. Sighs. Gathers her bags, rocks forward and lands on her feet, looks around, and wanders off in some direction.

She isn't overwhelmed today.

And neither am I.

# I Don't Want to Be Needed
## *David Gerson*

Right now I don't want to be needed. Not now. Maybe not ever. I will not lend an ear. Or a hand. There will be no shoulder to lean or cry on. I can't solve a problem. I don't want an update. I am not listening. Let me bask in a midsummer post-swim haze. Let me wallow in the smell of chlorine and citrus body wash. Let my skin be hot and cool. Let me squint to look at the sun. I won't read your email or take your call. I will not pivot. Please, don't circle back to me.

I will drink an Aperol Spritz in a real glass, one with a stem, and imagine that I am on the isle of Capri watching little boats filled with tourists as they head for the Blue Grotto. Or maybe I will imagine I am in Mexico watching the swimmers come in from the ocean, sun bleached and rough with sand. I am not able to do any favors. I am plumb out. I have no opinion. I ran out of those too. The new shipment will be delayed.

I will gorge on olives and artichokes, chips and salsa. I'll spoil my appetite because I can. I swear, I will eat dessert first. I have no suggestions. Or input. My well of ideas is bone dry. For once, I have nothing to say.

Let me be. Still and silent. Let my senses be heightened by each beautiful thing. But, please don't need me. Not today. I'm not available.

# II

# How We
# Survive

# This is How We Survive
## *Linda Laino*

You were a North Jersey boy, but a Southern man when our paths crossed. I was a Northern girl too, just eighteen and yet to feel like a woman. Did you consider your twenty-two years a man? I did then. What qualities of manhood does a twenty-two year old possess? Being far enough from childhood seemed enough. Warm breezes and the promise of springtime flowers lured us both south. Time was lush then.

Like an exotic bird, you excelled at attracting attention. Your color and form leaned toward the poetically absurd, and I peered into your world through my binocular glass with something like reverence. And why not? To me you had as much wonder as a creature who can fly.

Once, we sat under the moon on the shoreline of the river I lived on, LSD showing us the unseen world. The pulsating water patterns danced a thousand lights behind my eyes. "Let it play with you," you said, your voice rippling just like the water.

Play was your forte. Spontaneous as a summer storm, your life a lark. I swilled your adventures like water through a thirsty crack. Anonymity suited me in those days, but you needed to be seen. When everyone wore black leather, you wore white, topping your stork-like frame with punk attitude.

I showed up at your house when I felt you distant. I knew you weren't there, but I'd let myself in and go to your room. I'd finger your library and choose something I thought might please you. Sprawled across your mattress on the floor I'd read and wait. The moon waxed with the poetry in my hands while you leapt across the stars, outrunning your heart.

All the way north. Back to the Ramones and gritty clubs and practicing whatever avant-garde-fringe-thing you could pass off as serious work. I soon followed, feeling like I had reached the expiration of something.

I visited you in New Jersey and we fucked desperately in your car. You were different in New Jersey. Away from an audience, your party lampshade toppled off while the night shifted the soil under my feet. By the time my period was late, you were already gone.

Winter smelled like wood smoke and oranges. The cold knife of it went in and cut out a life. I drove that knife into a small corner of relenting earth. This is how we survive.

# My House
## *Brooke Davis*

Breathe in. Breathe out. People in. People out. My house is like a living organism that expands and contracts as its residents come and go, rooms change purpose, the seasons cycle on.

Nearly 25 years ago, I bought my house with my first husband. It was exactly what I wanted! A 4-bedroom brick Cape Cod with a fenced-in backyard. I fell in love with the post-World War II homes on Normandy Drive, as we attended open houses. They were in a great school district for our potential children, and the houses had good bones: hardwood floors, real tile in the bathrooms and the cutest little dormers to let in extra sunlight in the upstairs bedrooms. This one needed work but had four bedrooms. As I left the signing, I felt queasy. Was it nerves? We went directly from the signing to Westbury Pharmacy for a light lunch and a pregnancy test. In one afternoon, we decided to become homeowners and learned that we would be parents as well.

Alex came home with us to 1107 Normandy Drive on a sticky 100-degree day. He and I bonded on walks in the neighborhood and hours spent lying on a blanket in the backyard. About 4 years later,

Andrew came home from the hospital with us as well, and our family felt complete. I learned to garden and planted daffodils, irises, azaleas, and vegetables to enrich our environment and fill our bellies. I built a swing set for the boys, and we hosted numerous kids for playdates and birthday parties. Joe had been a house painter earlier in his life, so we painted each room of the house a vibrant color. Alex's room was a pale yellow while Andrew's room was a warm taupe. The living room was an orangey peach, the kitchen forest green, the dining room bright blue. Even the hallway leading up the stairs was sunflower yellow.

Ten years and 2 children later, this house was too small for us. Cozy had become cramped with a large German Shepherd, an ornery cat, two rambunctious boys, books, toys, and way too much furniture. We never could afford to renovate because most of our money went to kid expenses and home maintenance. No central air conditioning, no dishwasher, 1940s fuses that blew all the time; these flaws had become grating. Unfortunately, my husband's mental health took a serious turn for the worse. By 2005 he felt that a move to the country and a larger house would solve our problems. Our house was just supposed to be a "starter home," so perhaps it was time to move on? It felt like every crevice was congested. The tiny kitchen and lack of central air were miserable in the intense Richmond heat.

We rented a house near Ashland and put my house on the market. It didn't sell. The housing market crashed, along with our marriage, so in July of 2006, the boys and I moved back to our house, without their father. In preparation to put it on the market, we had painted the whole interior white, and moved all of our belongings out of the house. Now the house felt enormous! We returned with half of the furniture and none of my ex-husband's oppressive emotional baggage. Each of us picked a new bedroom and the boys, the pets and I created a new life here in what felt like a completely different house.

When Nick, my second husband, joined us here in 2010, we rented a POD® and for a month we sorted through our belongings, trying to decide which duplicates to discard and which pieces of furniture best fit our home. The next year we put on a new roof, added insulation, new windows, upgraded electrical service and added central air! The following year we knocked out a wall and renovated the kitchen. Nick and I repainted most rooms to a more soothing pallet of blues, pale yellow and lavender. Andrew wanted to paint his own room a silver grey. The boys completed elementary school, middle school and high school while living in the upgraded house. We hosted an endless stream of their friends. Nick and I expanded vegetable gardens and flower gardens. We played badminton and frisbee with the boys on summer evenings and dried wet camping gear from innumerable scouting and summer camp trips on the patio.

Alex left for college in the Fall of 2015 and returned the next Spring broken, addicted, and wearing an ankle monitor. Sometime that fall, I decided to reclaim the smallest bedroom in my house as a writing and meditation space. Nick and I painted it a soothing mint green and I filled it with my books, a desk and furniture repurposed from around the house. This became my refuge as we dealt with the storm of Alex's illness and had to send him away for treatment. Four years later, in Fall of 2019, Andrew left for college. Nick and I had the place to ourselves, and we really had no reason to go upstairs. Eventually, I turned Alex's old room into a beach themed yoga space where Nick and I could practice together or watch television.

In the Spring of 2020 COVID-19 arrived and Andrew was sent home from college amidst the unfolding crisis. We thought Andrew's return would last only a couple of weeks, but school shifted to completely online. For six months Andrew and I attended classes and meetings on separate floors. Andrew finally returned to campus in the middle of September. About 2 weeks later, Alex's roommate relapsed, and he was suddenly back in his old room after 4 years of living independently. My house became a sanctuary for the four of us and the boys' girlfriends.

My house is a small brick Cape Cod on a suburban lot. It is where I do most of my loving and living. It is my solace. It is home to my evolving family.

# My Father's Presence Everywhere
## *David Gerson*

I am not eating pizza topped with anchovies. The inside of my mouth is not tasting salt and brine. The tiny bones, as thin as a strand of hair, are not tickling my throat. The restaurant was out. And that's the whole reason I ordered from them. They have (had) anchovies. Not everyone has them. Domino's doesn't. Not in Baltimore. In Richmond, they do.

My fondness for anchovies came from my father. He loved them on pizza, on crackers, straight out of the tin. No one else in the family liked them. Just him. And me. It was something we shared. And I cherished it because we shared so little. Just the two of us. The others didn't get it. They were repulsed. When I eat anchovies now, I feel a little piece of my father is with me. The same with Claussen pickles. And chopped liver. And cheap lite beer in an aluminum can.

And I feel his presence whenever I wear a bow tie. It's like he is hugging me across time and space. He wore them all the time. So do I. His were clip-ons. Mine aren't.

And I have started to see him when I look in the mirror at my gray hair and in the gray stubble on my face. I see him in my expanding belly and in my fondness for seersucker suits, loud pants and louder shirts.

I think I hear him in my laugh, but I can't quite remember exactly what it sounds like. I think I do, but I'm just not sure. Memory plays tricks on me sometimes. There are pictures of his bright smile, mid-laugh in albums that have not been opened in years, maybe even decades. And sadly, photos don't come with soundtracks.

# Dad
## *Elizabeth Eley*

### Part I

My first memory of shopping with my dad was at the local Rose's department Store, circa 1972. It was fun Dad and I were going out; this was usually a Mom thing. I can still feel the smallness of my body then, trailing behind my father across the white tile floor as he strolled with casual purpose, always aware of my proximity to him. I asked why we were there; the options were endless. And really, what could Dad want or need that MOM hadn't already handled?

His exact words I can't recall but the shocking sting of embarrassment I felt is clear. Apparently Mom had sent him to replenish my cache of rubber pants. For those who don't know, rubber pants slipped over cloth diapers or cotton underwear to prevent leaks. This was especially useful during the adventure of potty training.

I was mortified. I tried to persuade him that Mom was the one who shopped for these. It was of no comfort he invited me to choose the colors I wanted (I did get a red pair). Clearly, my Dad must now know that I pee. That sometimes it doesn't work out in my favor AND what my underwear look like! I, of course, was overlooking the fact that the man had helped change my diapers for two years.

He was unfazed. He thought this was a fun outing. He probably even let me pick out a little toy or something but I don't remember that part. Just checking out, thinking the clerk now also knows I pee and hoping this type of trip never happens again.

## Part II

As a child too young to understand life and the power of her words, I declared to my father one day that I would commit suicide if he died. As though it were an act of solidarity. We were walking through some store together. My head just to the height of his waistband where he had tucked in a polyester blue shirt filling out my peripheral vision. He seemed shocked, which I thought was uncalled for, but he reacted calmly. It was one of those parenting moments I've come to learn, where words are chosen carefully in a fleeting second, for maximum impact. The delivery must be delicate so as not to warp them with a single exchange.

I sensed his caution. He explained he appreciated that I love him so much but dying wouldn't solve anything. I shouldn't give up my life for his. And later, if I ever thought I might, to just give it one more day. Promise him one more day, because whatever it is will always look different the next morning. And I have used that advice. I've done that for him. I honor him by living.

## Part III

"I just. Don't. Like it." she said, sitting bedside holding his hand.

In this moment of transition when her willingness to alter reality begs delaying its forced entry, she spoke the deepest intent of her heart. It was unrehearsed, traveling up wounded nerves to the swirling-numb brain, mouth firming words stating the obvious. The hope she could reverse it all with her raw power. The same strength she called upon to usher her mother from this world in peace and acceptance.

She was grateful to have been with him that entire last week. Grateful for the moment of lucidity they shared when he realized the sign he saw was an illusion. Pointing to the foot of the bed, "...you'll think I'm weird" he stated.

"I think you're wonderful." Love spilling over into his eyes, locked on hers.

With the feigned self-importance essential to his clever wit, Dad quickly retorted, "I think I'm wonderful too."

# Never-Never Land
## *Jer Long*

In the distance sat the clover-infested field where I smacked baseballs into outer space. Over that hill, we splashed in the cool Shenandoah River on blistering hot August afternoons. In the graveyard by the church, a few yards from ancestral headstones, I stood at Dad's grave. That's the moment I decided to return to Virginia.

Branded a Southerner, I couldn't scrub the South off my hide as easily as I combed the accent from my speech. Dad's Conservative staunchness, combined with Mama's Liberal obstinance, fueled the chemistry that is me.

A month after college graduation, my Mustang packed and my ambition itching to be scratched, I barreled down Route 66 to the promised land. It was 1980 and Washington, D.C. opened its arms to homosexuals such as me searching to live freely, openly, and honestly out loud. And so, I did.

"Blunt and opinionated, a Yankee like you could never come home again," a friend wrote to me in an email a few years ago. And yet, here I am, the return of the native from the land of milk and honey. A journey thirty-five years in the making.

Trapped beneath a bell jar of distress, my husband and I were confined to our Church Hill condo during the 2020 pandemic. I struggled to comprehend the events advancing around me. Our government spun out of control like a Hitchcock carousel. Ugly truths, once masked by polite indifference, were slashed by scally-wags eager to widen the chasm between the right and the left.

"A house divided cannot stand, "Abe Lincoln proclaimed. The foundation of our democracy was at stake. In a world where news was a selected service, propaganda fed an angry population. No longer the world leader of integrity and optimism, America fell from grace. Homespun, Norman Rockwell's illustration of an innocent United States was slammed mercilessly to the pavement. It gasped for air before it was riddled with bullets.

Being slam-dunked into the most consequential election of my lifetime, while witnessing the BLM events unfolding on Monument Avenue, I wrestled my demons. In the OLD SOUTH, I grew up in a family of misfits on the wrong side of the track. I grabbed at brass rings centimeters out of reach. One of six children, I dared to soar solo while tied to Mama's apron strings. Too often, I raced the wind down winding paths littered with roadblocks and detours leading to dead ends. That was a place called home.

In D.C., I created a new being from the crumbled pieces of a boy crippled by fear. Enduring Mama's "nervous spells," anxiety rendered me easy prey for bully bandits bilking camaraderie. Determined not to tumble off the edge of sanity, I picked at my flesh until a thread of silver lining was revealed.

Suffering "nervous spells," frightened and crippled, the POST-CIVIL WAR SOUTH rewrote its history. From disfigured shadows, manufactured mythical heroes were chiseled into stone gods and set atop mile high pedestals on an avenue designed to celebrate a fictional narrative and intimidate minorities. Shouldn't we know our place in the world? A myth repeatedly drummed into eager ears took root in ravaged souls. Inseminated with dishonorable traditions and reenactments of victorious battles, the ruling class, who raised Ole Dixie on flag poles planted before government institutions, legitimized Southern hypocrisy.

I was weaned on *Gone with the Wind,* fed fantasy pablum by a public school system propagating dreams, and bombarded with monikers for minorities sharp as pin pricks to the retinae of an eyeball.

Why? Because the truth was unbearable. When the stink of truth smacked hard the faces of the proud and self-righteous longing for what was, cowards, hidden beneath ghostly disguises, ambitiously crippled the meek. Fervently, they fed hate to their ravenous kin anxious to be villainous heroes. Decades past yielding little revelation, but deception, ingrained in the mindset, multiplied with each passing year.

The past was neither Robert Kennedy's liberal South that Mama dreamed of, nor the Eisenhower Conservative South Dad assumed he was living in. Nowhere existed a South for me or my minority allies. Justice was buried deep beneath the pillars of Jefferson's Monticello.

Shrouded in trepidation, we Southerners must rise from the muck and mire, as potent as COVID-19, to create a NEW SOUTH resplendent with equality legally protected by the law. Post-1960s riots, we gays molded Washington's abandoned Dupont Circle into a prosperous, inclusive neighborhood bustling with life.

Fantasizing about what must be, MY NEW SOUTH would be colonized by the colors of the human rainbow. Respect for one another's differences would flourish. Harmony would thrive. Being different would be an asset. Education would teach truth. Love would be love, no matter what one's class, color, sexual preference, or spiritual practice might be.

Thinking lovely thoughts, reborn Southerners would flit across a star-studded heaven with the Darling children. Wallowing in the golden glow of acceptance, we'd lounge lazy on the emerald lawn. Dancing shamelessly naked in the moonlit meadow thick with bluebells, we'd stumble into Never-Never Land, where children, rescued from condemnation, fly freely in the open air.

# Wine-Muddled
## *Alyssa Tyson*

In my earliest memory of my mother's alcoholism, we are in the kitchen, or maybe I walk into the kitchen. She throws up, or maybe she already had thrown up, and maybe I came in to help, because this is what it means to be the eldest daughter of 17- and 18-year-olds made parents overnight.

The puddle is wine-purple. Not red like blood, but the deep violet of the sparkling grape juice we always drink on New Year's Eve out of dollar store champagne glasses. My grandfather always loved it too, or maybe he didn't, I'm thinking now, because he was never at our house on New Year's Eve, and we always stayed home.

My grandfather—my dad's father—stopped drinking when he found out my grandmother was pregnant. She woke him from his fetal position in their long, gravel driveway to deliver her ultimatum: it was either the baby or the beer. In my mind, the way you forge a memory that isn't yours but feels like it is, she pokes him with a broom.

At 14, I stand in the kitchen and realize that a broom will not clean this mess.

The linoleum is still wine-dark. My father enters the room, a bundle of towels clutched in his arms. I think he uses them to mop it up. Mop it up, yes, because it's all liquid, as if the spill poured from the bottle itself, as if it had shattered. There should be bits of glass scattered here and there. When I, barefooted—no, wearing shoes, because I think we were headed to dinner—step carefully around where the mess once was, avoiding at all costs any contact with the still-sticky, unmopped floor, I am thinking of what it's like to step around broken glass.

Really my first memory of my mother's alcoholism should have been earlier, should have come with middle school, with finding plastic bags stuffed into my bedroom closet, clinking with the sound of empty peach-flavored Johnny Bootleggers. Back then, she said she hid them because my dad would be angry, or that she wanted to save them for an art project. And for years I believed her because I always saw the aftermath in the shape of my father's rage: strings of shouted swears rousing me from my sleep, shards of a kicked plastic trash can littering the hardwood floor, a coffee table overturned, a sunken heap of particleboard.

I never saw the negative bank account balances, the title taken out on the car, the guns and jewels and my Nintendo 3DS, the one I saved Christmas and birthday money for all year when I was eleven, pawned despite the 60 to 70 hour workweeks that drained the life out of my father.

When I asked her about the 3DS, after I'd noticed its absence, she said I must have left it with my grandparents, but I knew better. I never took it there.

# Cups
## *Kristi Mullins*

When I was in the fourth grade, my parents had separated. My mother rented a house not far from our home and that is where she, my sister and I lived. I continued to ride the bus after school to our old house where my dad would watch us until mom got off work. I don't think "bi-polar" is a diagnosis accepted or used in the mental health field today, but it's the term which best describes him. He had wild, manic highs and deep, debilitating lows. That made life with him unpredictable and often difficult. This was a low time. We would sit on the couch together under a blanket and watch *Capitol* and *As The World Turns* and *Guiding Light*. We would split a Coca-Cola between us. That was our ritual. He would pour the soda equally into two cups of ice. I remember the fuzz that would form on the cubes and the fizz tickling my nose. I remember leaving him notes to tell him I loved him because I knew he was sad.

My sister was born in 1969. At two months old she had exploratory surgery that uncovered a Wilms tumor on her kidney and her kidney was removed. Most babies with Wilms tumors at that time went undiagnosed and died. She was lucky to have had a persistent young doctor who insisted there was a shadow that shouldn't be there on her x-ray and requested permission to do the surgery. In puberty, she began exhibiting symptoms of epilepsy. She has suffered from depression since her teens. I remember her spending long periods of time in her room, in bed, with the lights off, watching her favorite TV shows and movies over and over. She would come out to get food or a drink. Her drink of choice is Sprite. She would take cups in, but they didn't come out. She amassed a huge collection of cups in her room. Every once in a while, my parents would instruct her to bring the cups down to the kitchen because there were none left to use. On her windowsill, the dresser, by the bed, under the bed. Once I found where she was urinating in empty cups to avoid having to leave her room.

My husband and my daughter both struggle with anxiety and depression. When you are depressed you save your energy for the critical tasks. The smallest things become harder. So, I am not surprised when I am the one who has to pick up the cups discarded around the house and take them to the kitchen. If I don't, they will sit there in perpetuity. Cold coffee growing mold. Sour milk. And I am the one who steps in to help clean-up my teenager's bedroom. Collecting forks and spoons, and cups. Because things become overwhelming and feel impossible. I know that feeling.

I have happy memories from my childhood. Every year we would attend the Oktoberfest and my parents would bring home two commemorative steins. We have a collection of steins from every year from the late sixties to the present. They sit atop a large bookshelf. After the steins came home, they were rarely used. They had a different scene each year and were colorful and cheerful. Years later I would collect steins of my own. Tradition is important to my mother. Every year you go to the Oktoberfest. Every year you decorate for the holidays and you use the good china at Thanksgiving. My favorites are the delicate water glasses with the etched botanical design or maybe the mismatched floral butter plates. My mother is a music teacher. For many years she has consistently created a gift for her students at the holidays. She orders music-themed plastic cups and fills them with candy and a pencil or fun straw. These are coveted by her students and past students don't forget them. They count on them. They count on her. My mother was our consistency. She was the stable and reliable one. The foil to my father.

I think everyone must have a collection of random plastic cups. Those cups you obtain from festivals and vacations and celebrations and work events. I shuffle and stack them just-so to fit in the cabinet. Beside the dry creamer, in front of the peanut butter. The Greek Festival fits over the Unhappy Hour at the Poe Museum which fits over the cup from my friend's wedding. If you keep them long enough, the writing gets scratched off or they crack or you leave them at your neighbor's house after the cookout. It's okay because you know you will get more. More events are ahead, more memories to make, more cups to bring home.

# Stubborn

## *Derek Kannemeyer*

What a docile little stubborn boy I was. I must have been eight or so. My parents were with a group of adults, one of whom made some kind of remark to which I answered that I didn't much care for girls. This provoked a certain amusement, especially when my father, with a knowing guffaw, turned to his assembled friends and wondered aloud how my position might change shortly.

I remember, I swear, resolving at that moment to show them all: I would not like girls.

But I had been, it would turn out, overconfident. I began, within three years maybe, to like girls quite a lot. Since I was stubborn, and had a problem with being wrong, it merely took me, what, another ten years to provide anyone in my family with any evidence of this fact.

A girlfriend took it upon herself (I was 19) to approach my mother at the store where she worked and introduce herself. I had, as she pointed out to me later, met her mother several times, and they didn't even live together.

I brought a girl home for the first time when I was 22. "Oho," my parents said, "so Derek's normal! Is Michael normal?" My older brother was gay, and neither out nor in: he, too, simply never spoke to them of such things. My poor parents. So sweet, honestly they were: merely so clueless. I remember also another family friend, when I was about 18, exclaiming to my mother what a handsome boy I was, and how many girlfriends I must surely have. And as my mother, in exasperation and astonishment, confided to her that I didn't have a single one, a stubborn eight year old still inside me smiled a little, to himself, revealing nothing to them, as if there was a great bet he had won.

# Forgive Me
## *Liza Kate Boisineau*

I am as old as my mother was when she sent me away to a mental health facility.

I didn't know I was going until I arrived home to find the nurses who'd come to fetch me.

My mom had packed a suitcase and I could see she'd been crying.

No, no, no!

I called her everything I could think of, but I wasn't dragged away.

I yielded, I caved, I sprinted to the van.

Fine!

I was twelve years old, but I couldn't throw things away or wash my body regularly.

My bed teetered and tottered on the ever-growing pile of things I would hide under there. There were bugs in my room and I'd put cigarettes out on the carpet.

I was asked to not come back to a kid's house down the street because I pretended to be possessed during a birthday party séance. Too convincing.

I threw a lizard into the neighbor's pool to drown it and each time I dove down to drag up its limp body it would start to breathe again, but it never tried to get away.

I finally threw it up against a wall over and over until it stopped responding.

I know I do not have to confess everything.

I know.

Not here.

I do not need to prove that I was bad to tell the story of my mom sending me away. For so long I did, though. For her, for the family. Just to explain. You see, I really was troubled.

***

The week before, she was late picking me up from basketball try-outs. Not very late, but the gymnasium doors had been locked and there were no cars in the parking lot and I had to pee.

I stood straight up between a low hedge and the brick gymnasium wall and went and went.

I did not pull my shorts down, I did not squat, I did not try to pee anywhere except for straight down my legs.

When my mom pulled up I ran to the car, sobbing.

She lined the seat with newspaper before she let me sit and we drove home in silence. There was an awful lot of silence back then.

We chatted on the phone for two hours last night, like old friends.

She's really quite funny and cute and the older she gets the more her New York comes out. It's charming and plain and I wish I'd really known her back then.

But we were on opposite sides of the moon, opposite sides of the universe really; two dusty objects, sharing a common atmosphere for a short while.

I don't know what I would've done if I'd had me to deal with.

I've made my claims over the years, I've rubbed her nose in it, I've begged for answers. I've lied and forgiven her; I've betrayed us both and taken it back.

Nothing made it feel better.

We don't talk about it, the family. It's a secret we're all ashamed of, I think.

None of that was my idea, my dad has said.

My sister, pregnant at the time, did not feel safe around me.

Her instincts were right, I wanted to hurt everyone. I'd already kicked her in the belly once.

I'd thrown forks at my cousin, I'd cut into my flesh, I'd screamed and drank warm beer in the woods and never knew a moment of mercy.

None for me, anyway.

My first night there, I shared a room with two 16-year-old girls. They were lovely to me, and I'm sure I embellished to impress them.

I'm a thief, I'd have said, which wasn't untrue, but it wasn't aggravated assault or a sex addiction or fraud.

They told me who to avoid, who to get cigarettes from, how to get out of doing schoolwork.

But after that first night, with no other girls my age in the program, I was assigned a room of my own.

A room with three beds, three dressers, three clock radios. Too much emptiness for only me, it just wouldn't do.

I scratched my arms up and told them I wanted to die so that I could sleep on a mattress in the nurse's station and spend my days on the couch in the lobby.

This was "suicide watch."

When everyone lined up in the morning for breakfast and class, I sat in my pajamas and made sure they knew that I was Bad.

Freddy spent his days in his wheelchair next to me. He drooled and watched TV.

Stay away from marijuana, the nurses said, this one became schizophrenic after smoking some bad stuff in Puerto Rico.

Freddy was the only adult patient in our ward, but he probably didn't know that.

For Thanksgiving, the group of preteen boys that had become my cohort and I all traced our hands and decorated them to look like fucking turkeys, my God.

We'd posted them on the shatterproof glass walls of the cafeteria so that when our families came for dinner, they could see what we'd done.

Like, to brag. Like, to show-off our "art."

*** 

Manic-depression, they said, when that was still a thing. Pills for a few days until a rash made my whole body bumpy and pink.

And then is a hazy moment of being held down by multiple nurses, wires everywhere.

Held down, struggling to be free, or just struggling.

Maybe they zapped me.

I stayed for six weeks. I was not "better" after six weeks, I was just no longer covered by insurance.

My mom, I know, felt she had no choice.

It won't surprise you to hear that I felt betrayed, abandoned, violated, hurt; there really is no end of descriptions yet none accurate enough to be complete on its own.

But it's not a competition. We were both lost, out of our depths, opposite and the very same.

I forgive me, I forgive me, and I forgive her.

# Remember Your Baptism and Be Thankful
## *Slats Toole*

I don't remember what day it was.

For a long time I thought it was April 16th, but that was actually the day of my baptism in a baptismal pool with a broken water heater, when I stood on a cinderblock shivering in a white robe after being dunked three times (Father, Son, Holy Spirit), trying not to sputter and cough because you don't spit up God's grace.

I don't remember what year it was, except that I was in fifth grade. The same year I was baptized.

I don't remember any precipitating event, but I think there was one, unless I have made up that detail to fit a narrative that is not actually mine. The decision was based on simple logic. I did not understand the purpose of living, so I would not anymore.

I don't remember why I tried water. It was not the foolproof choice, obviously, but it felt right, until my body realized what I was trying to do and fought to survive even when I didn't want to.

I do remember the prayer I prayed thanking God for my life as the adrenaline rushed through me and I coughed and sputtered and thought about my baptism. That maybe in this instance coughing and spitting was a sign of God's grace because God saved me, right? I do remember the shame I felt for that prayer for at least a decade after when I still didn't see the purpose of living but it felt like the door out was closed. The anger of, even for a moment, falling into this narrative I had already learned, that experiences like this lead to people realizing how grateful they were to be alive. A narrative that was not mine. I do remember the years of feeling like my body had held me hostage.

I do remember my later prayer, "God, if you want me to have this life, YOU use it."

I do remember going to school the next day like nothing had happened.

# Grinder
## *Louise Gilbert Freeman*

Right now, I am thinking about my teeth and night grinding. Yesterday I read in *The New York Times* that nightguards may be unnecessary and may even *exacerbate* grinding instead of diminishing it. But my nightguard and I go way back. I am terrified to be without it.

When I was in preschool, each time I petted my cousin's kitten, I clenched my five-year-old masseter muscles like a meth addict, my teeth gritting and skidding. Clenching staves off predatory animal-girl.

Spending the night with my best friend Jan in fourth grade, she said, "Lou, you were squeaking in the night."

At age 14, a dentist, examining my mouth, cheerfully announced, "So you are a bruxinator!" He hummed as he filed down my incisors to even out the chips, then he made my first splint. I was required to sink my teeth into trays of waxy, warm, bubblegum-pink, womb-pink gunk which they displaced so it oozed over the edges and onto my lips. I stayed like this for 20 minutes. When I was allowed to lift my teeth out of the pink, they made an ugly sound like *suck*.

I wore my first splint down in one year, sliding back and forth, back and forth until I chewed through it at the molars and the plastic became lace.

In college, my boyfriend thought he heard a small animal in the night.

In grad school I went to a charlatan, an alleged TMJ specialist who had me do isometric exercises, pressing my own palm against my chin and my chin against my palm. Then "the doctor" tried to take me out to dinner.

In Richmond, soon after I was married, I parked at an office lot in a parking spots whose parameters were marked by white stenciled and spray-painted molars the size of baseballs. This dentist fitted me with a tanner appliance, a splint fabricated on the mandibular arch. A few years later he replaced this with a smaller, sportier device that snaps over my upper incisors. I call it my "egg tooth."

A few years later I went to a local TMJ "expert" who, evaluating me, said, "Your jaw is askew and one of your shoulders is higher than the other. Moreover, your head is cocked to the left and your spine is misaligned." I felt like Quasimodo as I got back in my car.

The masseter muscle is the strongest in the body, exerting up to 250 pounds of pressure on the molars. My masseters are overdeveloped, Herculean, Popeye-esque. With immense, crude strength, they clench in maximum torquage each night. I think they could crush rocks, bust boulders, and certainly shatter teeth. I grind until my mouth is a blasted quarry, all detonated rubble. One morning I will open my mouth and all the bits I've crushed to powder will just fall out like cremated remains. I dream about my teeth, about them crumbling.

I am particularly fond of rabbits, perhaps because they literally *have* to chew all the time. They have open-rooted teeth that grow continuously — the Bugs Bunny front incisors, the molars, and the "peg" teeth. If the teeth don't get enough wear, they overgrow inside, their roots getting pushed back into the rabbits' jaws and skulls. A vet can shorten overgrown incisors with burrs on dental drills.

In recent years, I've been diagnosed with sleep apnea, a malady that requires a more complex mouthpiece. Yet another Richmond dentist has created something austere, medieval – a hinge-and-rod contraption that fits over all of my teeth. It thrusts my lower jaw forward, Neanderthalish. In the morning, I pop it loose and take it out, covered with spit, and finger it. Each plate is a long trough of canyons, jaggy ridges, craggy pits. It's like a raised relief map and the raised parts are very sharp, even after decades of grinding, back and forth, back and forth. I would have expected them to be two smooth planes by now.

Sadly, the sleep apnea device has made my TMJ so much worse that I have ceased using it and sought a new sleep apnea specialist. At my first appointment, his assistant created images of my mouth using a wand that is shaped much like an electric toothbrush minus the bristle attachment. It is hooked up to a large big-screen tv monitor. The assistant slid the wand around inside my mouth — laterally against my teeth and gums, starting at my lower left rear. The machine made a constant clicking, crackling sound like one might hear from a Geiger counter as it detects radiation, the sound you hear before you are sent for scrub-down. I have also heard this sound coming from my son's room as he destroys enemies in his video games.

As the assistant moved the wand, my teeth, horrifyingly, begin to appear on the big screen. My first thought is one of regret at not having bleached my teeth before the appointment for it now seems that I will have tea-stains and tannin-tints on my visual permanent record. I watch as the edifice of the upper and lower decks of my teeth begins to take shape on the monitor. The image reminds me of the Colosseum, rounded, tiered and imperial in scale. But it also has the excavated aspect of a Roman ruin since pieces are missing – tooth scanning is not a perfect process. There are holes where the wand has not been kept flush, and the gums terminate in ragged, post-apocalyptic indeterminacy.

When the dentist himself comes in, he sits jauntily on a stool, crosses his legs, and begins to reset my splint to its starting position with a tiny screwdriver and a magnifying glass. I say, "I bet you didn't think as a dentist you'd be doing the tedious work of a watch-maker or a jeweler." "You have no idea," he says. "Now with implants we use *tiny dental torque wrenches*." He enunciates each consonant very precisely.

"For jaw pain," I inquire, "does Botox help? And how is adminis-tered? Just one injection into each masseter muscle?" "Oh no," he replied, "It is twelve — in the jaws, temples, back of skull, base of neck." "Oooh," I say, "sounds like heaven."

# Invisible Actress
## *Theresa Ronquillo*

When I was in elementary school, my younger brother and I took the school bus every day. Our bus driver was a friendly older man who had driven the bus for decades. A lot of the kids called him by his first name, Lou. My brother and I addressed him formally, as our parents taught us to do: Mr. K. I saw Mr. K every day, twice a day, for nearly ten years of my life. In my memories he always had white hair and moustache, glasses, and a wool cap in the winter. He had an anchor tattoo on his forearm from his Navy days, and a loud booming voice that I can still hear over the din of exuberant children excited to go home after school.

One day when I was six or seven years old, I rode the bus home without my brother, sitting by myself on a brown vinyl seat in the middle of the bus. My house was only a couple stops after we left school, but that day Mr. K. drove past my street. When he got to the next stop, I thought ok, he made a mistake. He probably couldn't concentrate because the bus was so loud with kids talking, laughing, yelling. He's going to figure out his error, turn around, and swing by my house next.

But he didn't turn the bus around. He went to the next house, and then the next house. We kept getting farther away from my house. It soon dawned on me that I had been forgotten.

I was too scared to get up and tell Mr. K to take me home. It seems like such a simple action, but as a young child I was extremely shy and quiet. I was paralyzed with fear and couldn't move. Why couldn't I tell Mr. K, or alert another student who might be able to help?

I grew up sheltered and stifled, shaped by a familial and societal culture that exemplified the old adage of "children should be seen and not heard." I learned to not make waves, to not speak up, to stay small and invisible. I was too young to make decisions for myself and I certainly could not question the actions of adults, even if that meant being trapped on a school bus all afternoon.

The epitome of the quiet child with a huge imagination, I started envisioning scenarios. In one scenario, Mr. K finds me after the very last stop, cowering in a corner of the bus in the dark. He would comfort me, bring me to the front of the bus, and finally take me home at 6 PM. In another scenario, I imagined my brave self standing up, channeling my inner child actor, and shouting dramatically: "What about me?"

After cycling through different scenarios without acting upon any of them, I started crying. Perhaps that was my way of drawing attention to myself because I couldn't move or speak. Eventually, my savior — a very tall middle schooler — saw me, scooped me up in her arms, and carried me down the aisle while shouting at Lou that he had forgotten to drop me off.

Ten minutes later — or an hour later, or a lifetime — I was safely back at my house, my face streaked with tears, embarrassed and still shaking with fear. I never told my parents or my brother what had happened, for I was too ashamed and afraid of their reaction.

Weeks later, on the bus home with my brother, Mr. K. drove past our street again to the next house. My brother got up immediately to tell him that he missed our stop.

I'd like to think I stood up with my brother this time.

# Storytime
## *Amanda Riley Smith*

During preschool when I was four years old, my favorite time of day was when my teacher gathered us around for storytime. Her rocking chair creaked back as she sat down and we found our own spots on the carpet, gathered around her like baby birds in a nest. She kept the book a secret, held tightly to her chest, until we got settled. Then she flipped it around and revealed the front cover right before she started reading. Our anticipation growing, we could hardly wait until she panned the open book around after she read each page so that each of us could catch a glimpse of all of the pictures. Storytime in preschool was captivating and magical.

Until one day when my teacher read a story that scared me. I never wanted to hear it again. I became frightened at each storytime waiting for the secret book to be revealed. I kept my knuckles on the carpet and my feet flat on the floor and never quite sat down until she flipped the book around and I was reassured.

Then, it happened. "Boys and girls, today we are going to read "There's a Nightmare in my Closet" by Mercer Mayer. I was up and gone. I heard her saying, "Mandy, come back to the carpet," but I didn't care. I ran to the room next door, the organ room.

I crawled across the wooden pedals to reach the hollow organ bench. I tried to make myself smaller as I curled up inside of it. I covered my ears so I couldn't hear the story.

I didn't move. I could still hear her reading, but not the words. I still remembered what it was about anyway. A boy was very scared of the dark and had a nightmare living in his closet. The nightmare came out when the boy turned the lights off. The boy tried to make the nightmare go away. After realizing he couldn't destroy the nightmare, he decided to befriend it. In the end, the boy invited the nightmare to come and sleep in his bed with him.

When I heard my teacher get to the end, I uncurled my body and uncovered my ears, but stayed underneath the organ bench. She asked questions to ask the class.

Boys and girls, what can you do if you are scared of the dark?

Tell your parents!

Were the boy's nightmares real?

No!

That's right! Are your nightmares real?

No! Nightmares aren't real!

The class started snack time and my teacher found me, crying, rocking, sucking my thumb, twirling my hair and still hiding underneath the bench. "Mandy, what's wrong?" I just shook my head no. "Come here." She picked me up. My head rested on her shoulder and the breathy hiccups of a child's cry echoed in the organ room.

I didn't understand it all then, but I do now.

I was scared of the dark. My nightmares were real. And I couldn't tell anyone.

# Texting with a Radiologist
## *Sarah Twombly*

My husband texts, even though he knows I am working. He texts, hoping to make me laugh, not realizing that, since having children, every harrowing case he shares with me, I cannot help but imagine the patient is one of our two, tender-footed kids. This morning, he texts me the abdominal x-ray of a fifteen year-old boy that shows normal bowel gas with moderate stool, unremarkable bony structures—ilium, sacrum, pubis—and, as though it had been Photoshopped, a lightbulb in a place a lightbulb does not belong. My husband's text of the image is followed by an emoji laughing so hard it is crying.

My husband is chuckling out loud. I am sure, as he sends it, he is chuckling out loud, and all the other radiologists are chuckling too, because while I picture the fifteen year-old boy for whom a dare became a catastrophe, or for whom an experiment in adolescence went woefully wrong— who realized, slowly, over the course of a full and agonizing minute, precisely how wrong—and who then had to ask someone to help him, to see if, together, they could remove the offending object, and then when, even working together, they could not, this boy had to ask someone else, very likely his mother, to bring him to the ER, where he had to explain to an intake nurse, and then an ER nurse, and then a doctor, why he was there, if he was in any pain, if he could roll over, all while staunching his fear and grasping for the last few scraps of his teenaged dignity.

While I picture this, the radiologists are chuckling, because they know the lightbulb will cause no lasting damage to the muscle or surrounding tissue, because if the bulb was going to break, it would have already. And they chuckle because of what the x-ray does not show: a metastasized cancer, osteogenesis imperfecta, a perforated intestine. The lightbulb can be removed. They boy will recover fully, will be, in a few days' time, physically perfect again. The radiologists think, what a lucky kid.

I think about being fifteen, about driving permits and gym lockers, about sweaty palms and armpit stink, the embarrassment of tampons and hard-ons, the cliques, the snaps, the way a young heart sits in your palm and bleeds. I think, not everything is so easily excised.

I look at my husband's text—the image, this boy—and begin to cry.

# I Am No Monster
## *Linda M. Crate*

I remember once when I was with one of my exes he took me to a Halloween party he was invited to. He was friends with the hosts, so we stuck around after. There were a few different conversations taking place, and I'm not sure how we got to this topic someone mentioned how all babies that were resulted from rape should be aborted as they're all monsters.

As someone who came from such a violent beginning, I remember running to the steps on the other side of the room and crying. I always struggled to see myself as anything less than a monster, and this girl was basically confirming my fear that I was a monster no matter how good a person I strived to be or how much good I put into this world.

It really hurt my soul.

I am pro-choice, for sure, but I think people should be mindful of their words.

We don't need your brutal honesty. Where is your kind honesty, your compassionate honesty, your vulnerable honesty, your honesty that not only confronts but comforts?

The world is full of monsters, but that doesn't make me a monster. I am not my father or the horrible act that happened to my mother.

She was the one that once told me that "beautiful things can come from horrible circumstances." I knew she was talking about me. It brought me some comfort that she didn't see me as a monster because it is something that has nagged me my entire life. Am I a monster? Do I have a right to be here? Do I have a right to my dreams and ambitions? Should I be here, at all?

I hazard to surmise that I do. Because I am full of love, and there are those who love me. People should be able to choose for themselves what responsibilities and what choices they make without scrutiny or criticism, but please consider that you never fully know where someone comes from or who they really are. You could say something damaging to their mental and/or emotional health.

# Phạm Ngũ Lão
*Gary Kornfeld*

The place is Vietnam, Ho Chi Minh City in the neighborhood of Phạm Ngũ Lão. Phạm Ngũ Lão is a street in District 1 in Saigon and along with being a street it defines a neighborhood. I call it the ex-pat ghetto. I say ghetto not because it is poor or run down. Physically it resembles most neighborhoods in Saigon yet it is (or was when I was there) the center of great expat financial superiority. The expats wielded wealth most of their Vietnamese counterparts would never realize. It was also a neighborhood of a bustling economy.

It was riddled with shops, hotels, bars, spas, music stores, restaurants, travel agencies, tailor shops and assorted tourist businesses in addition to many street vendors, who peddled souvenirs, transportation, drugs, sex, gambling and any other vice one may wish to engage in along with assorted grifters and beggars, pick-pockets, small time thieves, hustlers and con artists. In Phạm Ngũ Lão it was very easy to indulge in one's addictions as local law pretty much turned a blind eye to foreigners' indulgences because their economic input was so pronounced. That grace, however, did not extend to all Vietnamese who supplied the foreigners. The authorities did step in when things got totally out of control or someone died. And foreigners dying in Phạm Ngũ Lão occurred more than one would expect. As previously stated, the same courtesies were not extended to all Vietnamese who proffered in the same vices.

I knew a woman who would traverse Phạm Ngũ Lão daily selling pot and who I was an occasional customer of. She was arrested for her transgressions and sent to prison. Upon her return to Phạm Ngũ Lão, she was reduced to depending on the kindness of strangers. Thankfully, mostly all her customers, of whom I knew many, gave her a dollar or two and she was able to eke out a meager existence selling worthless souvenirs or just asking for money outright.

Many expats lived in Phạm Ngũ Lão. I lived there for a while but then moved into District 10 and then later District 5. I knew some who never left Phạm Ngũ Lão except for brief forays as all they really desired from their life in Vietnam and HCMC was to experience as very little of it as was humanly possible.

I was a TEFL teacher and most nights I would work from 6–9 pm and after class I would go to the Santa Café located at Bùi Viện and Đỗ Quang Đẩu. Many of the teachers would meet there. The group was made up of alcoholics of which I was a card-carrying, dues-paying member in very good standing, drug addicts which I did not consider myself to be although I did buy and smoke pot occasionally (maybe three or four times a week), gamblers, sex addicts, and a few unencumbered earthlings as well. As far as addictions went, I was ok with most of them. How the other addicts felt about me fluctuated between acceptance and outright disdain. I was not a happy alcoholic camper. I actually got kicked out of an alcoholic bar in Nha Trang. The guy said to me, "Get the fuck out and don't come back." The only addicts that really rattled me were the sex addicts. They really alarmed me. They shook me to my core. I knew a few including a pedophile or two. What really unnerved me about them was their eyes. They all had these dead flat catatonic eyes. It felt like they were the walking dead, absolutely no one was at home. Wasn't nary a joke told by them, no sense of humor whatsoever. It seemed that all they were interested in was the next encounter. You could tell they had parts missing. VITAL PARTS.

When I would tire of the Santa Café and Santa Café and its congregants would tire of me, I would meander up Phạm Ngũ Lão past Đe Thám to Hem 28 Bùi Viện where there was a café whose name escapes me. It was like a second home to me and witness to many alcoholic dramas.

They had outside tables overlooking the hem and that is where I saw what I saw.

It was mid-afternoon around 2pm or so and I was already three beers deep into what would become a very, very long night when I noticed three Khmer children walking from the far end of the hem toward me. Khmer means Cambodian for anyone who does not know. Khmers were looked down upon by the Vietnamese. I guess every society, every fraternity, every group has another group they need to look down on, need to hate. We humans are very similar in so many ways. The peculiar thing about this group of children was that walking the lead was a young boy who was 8 or 10 years old. He was completely naked and smoking a cigarette. His right hand was placed at the tip of his right ass cheek and his left hand rested on his neck just under his ear and he would move it to his mouth and puff on the cigarette and then put it back. He was sashaying, primping, preening, peacocking down the hem.

The only way I can describe his walk is to say he resembled the show *Pose* or the movie *Paris is Burning*. He was walking a ball and his head would tilt from right to left and he would look you right in the eye and mockingly smile through you. And I imagined him saying, *I am Khmer. I am brown. I am dirty. I am 8 or 10 years old. I am completely naked and I am smoking a cigarette. I have a life expectancy of 12 to 15 years. And I am beautiful, so fucking beautiful. So, FUCK YOU. FUCK ALL OF YOU.* I was dazed and a bit stupefied by this procession and by the time I managed to gather my wits and reach into my wallet and extract a few bills he had already sauntered on by and turned-on Phạm Ngũ Lão and was gone. I ordered another beer.

I was kind of in shock. I turned to the alcoholic sitting next to me and asked him, "What is the meaning of life?" We alcoholics do wax philosophic inordinately. And the guy I asked was a very smart guy but alcoholic nonetheless. He looked at me and replied, "To create. All species, flora and fauna live to create more." I thought that made some kind of sense but it certainly excluded me along with many of the other alcoholics I fraternized with on a daily basis who had not created more, sired no off-spring. It made me wonder what my purpose was if I had not up to this point and had no plans in the future to create?

I became introspective. I turned to him and said, "Do you think I am a worthwhile human being?" And he smiled, kind of stared at me, uttered a small guffaw and laughingly said, "Probably not, but what does it matter?"

# Red Trauma
## *Amanda Riley Smith*

I hear it before I feel it. The whirring of helicopter blades chops through the dark air. Then the inevitable vibrations of the floor and the walls increase as the giant descends onto the landing pad.

I listen for the swish of the sliding doors opening at the same time as the movement from the propellers thrusts the crisp fall air inside. These puffs of fresh air seep under my door frame and breathe glimmers of hope and life into the staleness around me.

During these on-call nights, the bedside table lamp remains on. I rarely sleep, just rest. I am called to keep vigil over the hospital. I do not want to be paged to a person's trauma or to a dying patient and stumbling in the room without having enough time to wake up enough to be fully present.

In response to the helicopter transfer, my pager vibrates so excitedly that it jumps from the table to the floor. "Red Trauma: GSW (gunshot wound) v. female. ETA now" scrolls across the tiny screen. I get out of bed, straighten out my wrinkled clothes, check the mirror to make sure I don't have mascara anywhere on my face, pop in a piece of gum and say a prayer. I pick up my Bible and other Chaplain items and I take the elevator down to the Emergency Department.

At the edge of the trauma bay, I watch the familiar choreography of the trauma team dressed in their costumes of disposable yellow gowns and light blue bonnets with shoe coverings to match. In another setting and set to music, this routine is so well-refined that it might receive a standing ovation at the end. However, here the only finale desired is to keep this one dance from being final.

She is awake and crying. I join in their dance when there is the appropriate pause. I also know the routine. I hold her hand in both of mine. "Rebecca, my name is Amanda. You are going to be okay." I feel tubes being swung over my head. I bend down and duck like a child playing jump rope. The vitals nurse and I become dance partners as we trade places several times. I coo comforting words to Rebecca. When it is time for x-ray, everyone exits the stage.

It is then I hear policemen talking: A bunch of kids were at a party. Some accidental gunfire. This one got caught up in it. She's, uh, nineteen. Some underage kids there too. There were some other guns found on the scene.

Everyone rushes back to their places. Then members of the team leave, one by one, as their jobs finish. Just a few nurses and I carry out the finale. Rebecca seems as if she is willing her deep brown eyes to stay open. I touch my hand to her cheek, covered in dirt and fresh scrapes, and wipe her tears. She grasps my hand and attempts to speak. It comes out in just whispers.

I lean down to her. In a dry, broken voice, she speaks slowly and painfully, swallowing after every word. "I think my boyfriend shot me. I can't feel my legs. And what about my baby? I'm pregnant.

We were fighting about the baby."

God, I have no words. But please help me help her.

The nurse whisks her into an awaiting elevator. I am left alone in the middle of the empty trauma bay with the remnants of the last dance littering the floor. I take the pager off of my belt to check the time. The trauma alert still scrolls. I silently correct it in my mind. Red Trauma: GSW v. female and baby.

III

# Letting Go

# Indoctrination Training
## *Derek Kannemeyer*

Apparently, the members of my favorite band were now all Scientologists! I knew too little at that time, in 1970, in Bournemouth, England, for this revelation to dismay me, although it worried me, and it baffled me. I had assumed Scientology was crazy shit. Could I be wrong? And what would it do to their music?

At 20, if I worshipped anything, I worshipped the Incredible String Band. Those first four (pre-Scientology) albums—wow! So— out of curiosity, not expecting or fearing that I might be converted— I signed up for Scientology classes. Four Saturday afternoon sessions. I considered myself well-armored. I suspected going in that the experience would be completely nuts, and maybe a little sinister. Well, I would be ready.

In the event, I was disappointed. Oh, it was all as crazy as I thought it would be, but the movement towards indoctrination was so leisurely. We did get lent books, that goofy dianetics mumbo-jumbo. We were, in the casual conversation at each session's intro and outro, tossed a few crumbs of the large claims—that the future of the world was a race between Scientology and the nuclear bomb;

that a fully clear Scientologist could, oh sure, overcome most kinds of death; that yeah, we could be put in touch with our past lives, if we signed on and pitched in enough money. But we were to leave all that aside for now.

Instead, in facing pairs, over the course of four two hour sessions, we did exercises in just being. For half an hour, taking turns, we were to sit serenely, and to strive to unseat a partner's serenity. I was good at the serene sitting, but uninspired and inconstant as a pesterer. We were not allowed to touch, or to threaten touch, but otherwise anything (supposedly) went. My classmates were mostly as cordial as I, so that nothing much did go. The verbal assaults were sporadic, and there was no even mild exhibitionism. One guy's best line, I recall, was "Whip me with a wet bra," which made a whole row of girls snort and giggle. I stayed serene.

For the second half hour, one partner would ask, "Do birds fly?" then "Do fish swim?" until the other one said, "Yes." No other answers were acceptable. The script for any reply but "Yes" was a patient "Let me ask it again. Do birds fly?" Or else, "Let me ask it again. Do fish swim?" It sounds creepy now! It sounded creepy then. And yet when it was my turn to ask, I asked until my time was up. I was good at it. I was relentless.

Sometimes, when I was asked back, "Do fish swim, do birds fly?" I took pity, I answered "Yes." Sometimes I gave wiseass responses; wiseass responses were fun for a while, although that "Let me ask it again" as the counter to every last one of them did get annoying. Sometimes, and after four weeks I was expert at this posture, I wreathed every exposed, soft human inch of me in stillness, and I sat unyielding and serene, just being.

# Small Talk
## *Courtney Allen*

When I smile I'm saying hello and by that I mean I'm terrified of how close we'll end up and by that I mean telling you my name and learning yours too, because a split second after the fact I'll become giddy at how your name tastes on my tongue. Then I'll be fighting back tears because once my imagination sprints a mile a minute with your name in it we won't become anything. It's the inevitable pattern I follow all the time on accident, and I can't do anything except stand and let my heart take the hit. I'll want to stop there but what if you ask me to dance? Of course I'll have to confess that I don't know how.

When I say I don't know how to dance I mean I don't know how to have a comfortable conversation with a stranger and by that I mean eye contact and by that I mean intimacy and by that I mean have you ask about me and by that I mean tell you my story and at this point I'm praying.

When I say praying I mean panicking and by that I mean begging and by that I mean demanding God LOOK! I don't believe in signs anymore so show me the truth even if it squeezes the love out of my lungs; we're figuring this motherfucker out right now. And by that I mean figuring out how much room I should make and for how long. And by that I mean do I tell you that singing was my first love or that I've never been in love? Hopefully you keep it safe and ask what I like doing. You'll learn that it's reading.

When I say I like reading I mean disappear and by that I mean hopefully for good and by that I mean I hope you won't remember me because let's face it I won't be who you hold in your head and I hate disappointing people. And by that I mean being myself and by that I mean weird and by that I mean quiet and by that I mean observant and by that I mean I will question every move you make towards me while I count how many exits this room has. You'll grow exhausted from all this; trust me I am too.

When I say exhausted I mean I can't hold on to you, but that doesn't mean I don't want to.

# How to Grieve an Alcoholic
## *Marie Marchand*

I can't remember his high school and college graduations. I can't remember his wedding and the birth of his children. I can't remember his plein air watercolors and his abundant summer gardens. No matter how hard I try, I just can't. Because they didn't happen.

I try to fill this absence with imaginings of my brother having had a life beyond the bottle—beyond the beer, peach Schnapps, and wine with which he numbed and slowly killed himself starting way before his death yesterday at age 53.

How do I remember him if there are not touchstones by which we commonly mark our lives?

Only a small part of me is grieving my brother's unrealized accomplishments and successes. What I'm really mourning is the absence of those typical experiences of a life well-lived. Those soothing consolations that give life its meaning: beauty, connection, belonging, and acceptance. The Dalai Lama said, "Love and compassion are necessities, not luxuries." Addiction withheld these from my brother. Why was he exempt from these gifts that should be the birthright of everyone?

"Blame" needs to have its own stage in the five stages of grief because that's where I am right now. In the last 24 hours, my mind has thrown darts of blame at a number of people, including myself. At this moment, my target is the manager of the Westminster AMC Theatre 36 years ago who fired my then 18-year-old brother for eating leftover hotdogs in the alley before dumping the concession trash. This was the month after my brother won AMC Employee of the Month. I'd gone to a movie I didn't even want to see just to witness my brother's photo on the big screen. He was proud of that accomplishment. The manager couldn't have disregarded the hotdog incident? Couldn't have offered my brother a second chance? Now look what's happened! This is all that manager's fault.

Big brothers can go either way. Some take on the role of protector; others not so much. Growing up, mine was a bully. As a little girl, I shoved my feelings inside, until I learned the f-word and threw a heaping plate of spaghetti and meat sauce onto his lap. For my own mental health, I moved away after high school.

Then, in 2005, I let it all go. All my anger and resentment drained away when I saw him lying in the bed addiction made. I encouraged him incessantly to try AA. I even called AA myself. When I said I was calling on behalf of my brother to find out how I could help him, the person replied, "You can't." I thought that person was callous. "I'm educated and resourceful, I said. Of course I can help him!"

My brother mellowed over the following 16 years as his body and spirit weakened. He isolated himself from everyone and spent the last decade sleeping and drinking. Drinking and sleeping. His meanness towards me mostly faded.

Now that he's gone, I want to recall only the good stuff—those times when his best-self showed up, those rarities for which a person should be remembered, even if those moments were from 40 years ago. I want to focus on his unalterable humanity.

My favorite memory of my brother, other than making snow forts together in Colorado, was his choir concert at Bill Reed Jr. High when he performed a duet of "Up Where We Belong." He wore a tie. He was smiling. He had pictures taken with my uncle and my mom. He was a star.

Addiction took my brother down that harsh road of slow deterioration from cirrhosis and the dizzying hepatic psychosis that comes from decades of daily drunkenness. Over the past five years, every time my dad called, I thought it was the call where he would softly say, "Marie, I have some bad news."

I finally got that call yesterday.

For 35 years, my brother wore the false identity of addiction to alcohol. But that's not who he was. Even his personality, a humor that somehow survived through his struggles, was not who he truly was. He was part of the self-expression of universal light temporarily manifest in human form. Now, he is free from the cruel stranglehold that limited his life here on Earth. Now, he is lifted up by love to where he belongs.

Now, he is limitless.

# Ang Walis (2020) (Broom)
## *Theresa Ronquillo*

Yesterday I bought a walis from an Asian grocery and supply store.
Not an "authentic" one made in the motherland
But nonetheless a broom that I can sweep the floor with
Using one hand.

I had read somewhere that during this time of COVID-19
We are encouraged to go to the smaller ethnic grocery stores
Instead of the big box supermarkets.
It did cross my mind
That people might avoid Asian stores
Because of their racism.
That we might be left alone while we shopped, walked, lived.
(Update: I was wrong. They don't avoid, they attack.)

When I swept the floor this morning with my new walis
A childhood memory popped in my head

Of dressing up as a witch for Halloween when I was in second
grade

Black hat

Black cape

Black Izod shirt, black pants and shoes

Black lipstick

And a walis

The only kind of broom we had at home,

The only broom I was familiar with

And because white suburban kids

Were total assholes

They laughed at me and my walis and made fun of me

"What's that?"

"That's a broom?!"

"What kind of broom is that?!"

"You and your family are so weird!"

(I made that last statement up. Maybe.)

I was ashamed

I was mad at my parents for sending me to school

With a Filipino broom

I just wanted to fit in.

I just wanted to be a normal witch.

I just wanted a normal broom.

When I thought about that Halloween memory
The phrase "they avoided me like the plague"
Also popped in my head.
The childhood reality
Of internalized anti-Asianness.

But because writing is healing,
And growing up happens,
And learning to love myself happens,
I re-framed.

Back in second grade,
I might not have had the language to articulate
my feelings of shame
Or the power, or the agency, or the thick skin.

But I do now.

I am a powerful witch. Sweep.
A bruha. Sweep.
Sweep. Sweep. Sweep.

I have the power to transform.
Shapeshift
Fly

Are you afraid of me?
I am no longer afraid of you.

# Emergence
## *Lois Henry*

Sometimes you just need to dive into the unknown. I've been reminded of this on recent foggy mornings as I cross the James River on my commute to work. The cars ahead of me vanish into the mist that has enveloped the roadway. It looks as though the entire bridge has disappeared, that I am about to drive into nothingness, plunge into the water below.

Roads, especially mountain roads and bridges over water, have been scaring me lately. I can't seem to drive over a bridge without feeling tense. I remember my panic attack on the Bay Bridge in Annapolis, fear suddenly rising in me, immobilizing me, the pressure in my chest, my palms sweating on the steering wheel, my car creeping slower and slower toward the peak of the bridge. I talked myself across by praying the Hail Mary on repeat, 24 Hail Marys in all. I think of a man I know, driving over the edge of an overpass after drinking too much wine, falling to the highway below, killing his wife and injuring his son. I think of others dying while standing on the shoulder of the highway, beside a car disabled after hitting a deer. The drive over Afton Mountain also troubles me, the long curving incline, the guardrails separating me from the steep drop to the valley below, the narrow two lane road with the "look out for falling rock" signs. One gray November afternoon, I passed a car on fire near the top of the mountain, was forced to drive past the scene in the next lane, no shoulder. I expected an explosion, the thing that would push me into the rock wall, or plummet me over the edge.

I don't want to invite tragedy, but wish I could be more willing to let go, to embrace the unknown and face down my fears. I tend to crave comfort, security, surety. I find peace in routine, organization, the familiar. But recent events have made me long for some risk, and perhaps, even a bit of danger. I have spent too much time lately contemplating lives lived in fear of the unknown, observing people who have imprisoned themselves in elaborate dungeons of their own construction, surrounded by possessions and memories, cobwebs and dust. I have seen what happens when those people run out of time, when that prison becomes a life sentence.

Perhaps, when I throw myself into the unknown, I won't return, or I will return as a person changed. But what I have found, on those foggy mornings when it is my turn to cross the bridge, drive into the fog itself, that things come into focus and the mist fades. I emerge on the other side of the cloud, on solid ground.

# Who Is Sid Jordan?
## *David Gerson*

Right now I am thinking about Sid Jordan. Sid Jordan who I met on SCRUFF over the weekend. SCRUFF, which tells you how close someone is to you by the foot and that they are ready to fuck. Is that what Tinder is like? Sid Jordan, who may be called that after Sid Vicious and who may be 51, though he looks older. Sid Jordan who was born in Ireland and raised Catholic by parents who probably hated the sin and loved the sinner. Amen. Sid Jordan who married old and became a widower young. Sid Jordan who kissed me open mouthed in a trendy restaurant I do not frequent on our first and only meeting. Sid Jordan who put his hand firmly in my lap as I perused brunch selections on a menu in my phone because paper menus are germy. Sid Jordan with whom I shared a meal that was like a sprint, instead of a stroll. Sid Jordan who ate fast and undressed faster. Sid Jordan who wore sexy underwear because I told him it turned me on. Sexy underwear that looked better on the floor next to my bed than it did on him. And it looked really good on him. Sid Jordan, to whom I said foolish things like, "I think I'm in love," as I kissed and washed his back, even though I'm not. In love. Sid Jordan of Marblehead, Ohio, 40 minutes from Toledo, by way of Mallorca and St. Marten and Nyack, New York and Key West and 40 miles outside of Dublin. Sid Jordan, who asked how far I lived from Pittsburgh because it was in the middle and maybe we could meet there some time. Some day. "Four hours," I said. And "sure," I said. We could meet there. One day. Sid Jordan who I sent off with a kiss and a squeeze on the backside and a wink that said, I'm old enough to know I will never see him again.

# A Guy Named Patron
## *Nikiya Ellis*

I used to use tequila to get me through the lonely nights,

High heels and tight dresses on the wet warm cobblestone streets,

The "hey beautiful" and "damn girl,"

Never made me feel beautiful,

The smell of smoke and trap music made my stomach question
my mind,

It was just me and my girls though,

Secret conversations over loud music,

Greasy lips from fried chicken,

"Walk with me to the bathroom girl,"

Admiring the beautiful melanin filled stalls,

Tattoos, expensive bags and gold hoops,

Would he be here tonight?

Fuck him,

Give me two shots of Patrón and a Red Bull,

Last call & I still couldn't find him,

Or was I even really looking?

Shit, glass is empty,

"Girl come on are you drunk?"

Was the last thing I remember as I rolled my eyes and realized I did it again...

I spent another night in another bathroom, head in the toilet after drinking way too much. Looking for love in the club but ended up finding a guy named Patron who was the most abusive relationship I had. No I wasn't an alcoholic but did I use it to get me through some tough times? Of course I did. Did I use it to make the club more tolerable? Sure did. The phone rang and on the other end I heard that voice, the same one I tried to drown out last night, the most hypnotizing tone I've heard all night "Can I see you tonight" hell no I thought but my womb screamed yes. Yes he can see us, he's better than tequila and I know you don't want to go through this two nights in a row, I agreed with her. I gave in again. "Fuck him." I thought and I did just that.

# A Love Manual for My Ex
## *Cecelia Meredith*

Post Sender: Please see enclosed letter for instructions on the boyfriend I am returning. He didn't come with a love manual so please understand the painstaking work that went into this.

Post-post Sender: Please also note that this was an ongoing project until recently.

My ex-boyfriend didn't come with a love manual. He came with a credit card that has his name on it, attached to his parents' bank account, and long blonde hair. He came with soft eyes and rolling bags that he unpacked neatly all over town. Occasionally I see some of his dirty laundry when I'm on my way to work, but my heart doesn't hurt anymore.

For his convenience, pack yourself neatly into that rolling bag once it's empty, but don't hope for much because he won't hold on as tightly as when his own things were inside. And he'll try to make you "his thing," while trailing you on a leash ten steps behind. You'll love it. You'll love being the period at the end of his sentence and the footnote of his life. Regardless of your own experiences and self-love, you'll always be second.

Second to someone, though, is first to him — except you won't be.
You'll be fourth or maybe fifth, behind his mother, his brothers, his
fraternity brothers, his new Xbox, and his phone.

Cater to his whims though, because they'll make him smile and God
that smile will drive you until it drives you right off a cliff.

I called myself a box person once, because I wrapped myself in pretty
pink paper held together by ribbons and crooked staples that
reminded me of the picture that hung from our wall in the first
place we lived together. His temper got the best of him in those
days and I stopped adjusting the frame.

Because of that temper he learned to breathe deeply instead of rush
in like a waterfall. So he'll pause for you like he never did for me
because my words weren't precious until I was telling the world
just how broken he truly was.

And I held him together with bear glue that turned to sand and
slipped through my fingers until it was my problems that needed to
be suffocated but there was no courage to be mustered from his side.

So you'll fight the good fight to shape a boy into a man,
just remember not to lose who you are in the end.

# The Things I Never Told Him
## *Alyssa Tyson*

"What I haven't told you is I hate your roommate and I might also like girls" is the conversation I'd wanted to have with my ex-boyfriend the day he broke up with me. I had been stewing over both of these things for months, wanting to ask him if maybe one weekend, just one, his roommate would leave us to ourselves, or maybe we could leave his tiny apartment and walk around a park. I would tell him about the girls I kept seeing on TikTok, how I caught myself watching their videos on a loop, 60 seconds repeated and repeated and repeated, how I had caught myself staring at a few girls like this since high school. I would tell him that probably it meant nothing, that I was still straight because it was impossible not to be; surely everyone sometimes thought about kissing girls every now and then.

"What I haven't told you is that you drink too much," I would tell him. Every weekend, I lost track of the crushed beer cans he'd toss into the recycling bin overflowing in the corner of his unkempt living room, the mountain of them overlooking a sea of dirty bongs and books I had never seen him pick up, not once. I kept loving addicts, none of them in recovery.

"What I haven't told you is that I hate the way you talk to me sometimes, like I know less than you. Like I am less than you." Like how I opened a bottle of soy sauce and he'd shouted at me because there was already one open. When I pointed out that it was teriyaki, he checked behind me, untrusting of my capabilities to read the peeling label. I wanted to tell him that it wasn't my fault his roommate lacked basic adult living skills, that his roommate had floated from woman to woman to his best friend, eventually, weaponized incompetence brandished and blazing.

Before I could say any of these things to him, he paused the TV—the same stand-up comedy we'd watched a week before, because he'd been too drunk and too stoned to remember any of the punchlines. Each time, he laughed at them as if they were new.

He wasn't laughing when he turned to me and said, "I think we need to have a conversation."

# Jack, I Swear
## *Hope Whitby*

*for Elizabeth F.*

It's a savage twist how these wildflowers,
centuries-old, now, cultivated to behave,
have their turban folded petals feather
into daggers of flames. The tendrils of their blooms
blaze upwards into wispy skies and spreads rampantly
across glazed blue and white China plates.
What creates them, this passion - is what kills them.

Ennis Del Mar came in from the cold,
falling into the warmth of another man's body
designed like his own, strong and yearning, and
what he came to understand while being held
in Jack's embrace is — this is living. As long as
they stayed on the mountain, away from the world —
living was loving.

But cowboys are born to roam, Ennis and Jack

returned to fantasy leaving behind their reality

which became reduced to brief reunions arranged

by coded postcards. The open range becomes small

when love is confined to secrets and when secrets were revealed,

Jack's light was extinguished by hands of hate determined

to destroy flowers that bloom different from their own.

Let me tell you about this tragic love story's

last gasp of sacred beauty. Layering his shirt

over Jack's, Ennis placed them on the same hanger.

As he wept into the woven flannel threads,

Ennis spoke aloud,

Jack, I swear,

you're no broken tulip.

# Rio's Girl
## *Melissa Face*

I am in love with a gang leader.

His name is Rio, a character portrayed by Manny Montana in NBC's *Good Girls*.

Maybe I'm just infatuated.

Would it still sound weird if it were simply lust? I mean, show me a straight female who hasn't wanted a bad boy at some point in her life. It might be the fast car, the scent of danger, the involvement with something illicit. You know it's happening, but you can't prove it. He can't be outed.

That's not it for me, though. Not this time.

Sure, his neck tattoos are sexy. His car gets my adrenaline pumping. I like that he meets Beth at night in the park and how he sneers and licks his lips when he dismisses her excuses.

Beth should know by now to not disappoint Rio though, right? Print the money. Move the hot tubs. Sell the stuff, for God's sake.

Do what he says! And what do you get in return?

His Loyalty.

That's the part I tried to explain to my mom the other day.

"I'm going to write about how I want to befriend a gangster,"
I told her.

"Oh! So you're writing fiction now?" she asked.

"Nope."

"So what are you saying? Do you want to join the Hells Angels or
something?"

I told her I didn't. I don't know how to ride a motorcycle.

I'm also not interested in money-laundering, trafficking, drug
dealing, or any other type of organized crime. I'm looking for the
bond of a fellow gang member.

I want to know how it feels to be on the inside, to be vouched for,
to be defended.

Rio would do that; I know he would.

I have wondered how things would have turned out if he had been
there for me in the past, the times I really needed him.

What would he have done when my boss at the surf shop commented
about my chest size, asked me to perform "extra duties," and fired
me when I didn't comply.

How would he have responded when the crazy lady pointed her
finger in my face and shouted obscenities at me?

What would Rio have done when I was cast out by every member of my family?

I imagine he would have "taken care" of those who wronged me. A simple, but terrifying threat would have sufficed.

"I heard you upset my girl, Melissa," he would have said. "Are we gonna have a problem?"

"No. There's no problem. And it won't happen again," they'd say.

And it wouldn't. Because everyone would know that I have him in my corner. More importantly, I would know that someone is in my corner. I would feel it. The feelings I have longed for all of my life — protection and belonging.

It's really not that sexy after all, is it?

It's familial.

"You can't hurt me anymore," I say. "I belong to Rio. I'm his girl."

# Cherries
## *Linda Laino*

My local fruit market was selling cherries today so I bought a bagful. Eating cherries reminds me of my father. Walking home, I saw him standing in our 1970's burnt orange kitchen, his back outlining the window against the thrum of the air conditioner. Behind him the glint of the metal colander in the sink, filled to the brim with the shiny, wet fruit. They seemed like the Rolls Royce of fruit to me as a child, since he always announced their arrival in a special voice. "I've got cherries!" he'd singsong with a wink, as if it was a covert snack. I only remember the two of us ever eating them in my family.

Before I grew into a wannabe hippie teen who clashed with his conservative values, I remember my father and me as "pals." We have similar tastes and temperament and everyone said I looked the most like him of his four children. He doted on me and over the years we shared a secret or two: teenage transgressions with boys and drinking on my side, the same, with middle-aged women on his.

My father is now nearing the end of his life. He lives alone at 91 and with failing health, he is tired. I feel it in his voice. A voice that terrified me as a child. He was a yeller then, needing to be heard over four kids and a dog. But his anger was something that burst like a firecracker, then dispersed into playful teasing or offer of something special, like cherries. Even though now, his voice is losing its spunk, he is lucid and philosophical, ready to "check out," as he says. I want to offer solidarity, but agreeing with his death seems wrong.

"Tell me something you remember about me as a child," I say. His nostalgic grin not missing a beat, he launches into a story of losing me on a crowded summer beach when I was three. "I looked up and you were gone! I later found you roaming the boardwalk, as if you were on a tour of the town, just taking it all in." He seemed delighted to find me in that state, and I like to think he followed me for a while—letting me wander—before scooping me up.

"You were never a good sleeper," he says, telling me another story. "You had devised a way to climb out of the crib and slide down the wall to the floor." A feat my son would perform many years later. Mother and son escape artists. My father thinks this took great intelligence and smiles with pride as he thinks back to my toddler ingenuity.

Food was love in my Italian family, especially with my father. He owned and operated a deli and catering business and loved to cook. Since he often proclaimed me his "best eater," I'd wait in anticipation on summer days for his return from the Italian market with delicacies like cannoli and cheesecake. And cherries. Stone fruited skins, stained, bloody fingers; juicy spits of pits into our hands. We'd make a pile of them with the stems, sweetly chewing our way through summer.

Eating cherries with my father. At the kitchen table, the big bowl between us like a shiny purple mountain. I am looking up at him, so I must be small. Is this a memory? Or did I see it in a photograph? Is there a difference? Gauzy monoprints on paper merge with distorted remembrance. A big protective hand, a shoulder that smells like a scented envelope I slip into.

I am sitting at the piano, age nine. My feet can't reach the pedals without a slide forward. "The falling leaves drift by my window…" peals from my fingertips as my father stands singing and turning the sheet music. He puts his hand on his heart for the high notes.

"He's going to survive us all," my mother used to say. Even though his first heart attack occurred at 45 and he has had a multitude of hospitalizations and health issues ever since, that prediction of hers has turned out to be true. Did you know that cherries, the heart-shaped fruit, have properties that protect the heart?

He sits looking like a bobble head doll, his head larger than the rest of him. It hangs low, his enormous, sad eyes protruding. It must be the newly lost weight I think. My sister dislikes this hang-dog look. His "puppy-eyed face" she calls it. She thinks he perfected it to win our sympathies after he left our mother. But I was never as hard on him as she was. The sister who would remind me that I left and she stayed; saw the deception, the lies, the toll on my mother. I allow my breath to soften this knot between us like the pass of an olive branch we have extended to each other late in life.

On the phone today, my father doesn't sound like a dying man, but suddenly rather animated. I want to treat him like he's dying, but I'm not sure what that should look like. Do I feel obligated to have reverence for the moment? My old Catholic coming out. But he refuses to be somber about it. He assures me he is ready.

Organs are failing. The amount of energy it takes to do simple things is starting to frustrate him. With shrinking activities and everyday tasks harder to perform, my sister offers hospice and despite his initial refusal, now he says, "I'm ready to go." Older, traditional Catholics believe there is a heaven. An actual place you will float around in forever surrounded by benevolence. Both of my parents shared this belief. My father believes that my mother is waiting there for him. Maybe he thinks hospice is one step closer to heaven.

When I call him these days I want to ask questions: Will you tell me a boyhood tale? What was the happiest time? The worst? Why did you leave my mother? Do you remember telling me I was your favorite? Can I bring you some cherries? But I am mute on these points. We talk about music and how he will be happy to have WiFi again in hospice which means Nat and Frank back in his airwaves. I make a mental note that their music must be played at his funeral service.

Sorting through his things, he wonders if he needs to take his pots and pans to hospice. "No," my sister tells him. "They will have everything there." He seems relieved. In fact, he seems relieved about all of it: the leaving of possessions, the moving, the dying. Death is close enough to smell now. She is suddenly shadowing his days. I wonder if he yearns to sleep young in green fields again, get away with petty crimes, and make-out until his lips ache. Or maybe that is my list.

How is a life filled? Behind my eyes, an image downloads from nowhere—or from everywhere—thousands of cherry seeds winnowed and blown, each contributing a pixel, until a scene appears, fully-formed like Aphrodite from the head of Zeus: A summer day, a bowl of ripe cherries, a feeling of rightness. Was it enough? Your life?

# Author Bios

**Courtney Allen** is a writer from Missouri who writes poetry and prose. You can also find her blackout poetry on Instagram under the handle Readsandsips.

**Liza Kate Boisineau** lives on and off the road with her partner and their dog. She is a writer of songs and of true stories, and is an aspiring potter. She has a happy life now that she knows there is enough to go around.

**Priscilla Cash** finds herself living, working, and writing in Richmond, VA. She's been a professional rock climber, dorm parent, waitress, nurse, pharmaceutical sales rep, and fundraiser. She likes to grow things, rescue orphaned orchids, foster kittens, and make music with the people she loves.

**Linda M. Crate's** works have been published in numerous magazines and anthologies. She is the author of seven poetry chapbooks, the latest of which is: *the samurai* (Yellow Arrow Publishing, October 2020). She has also authored three micro-collections, and four full length poetry collections.

**Brooke Davis** is a school librarian, part time mindfulness coach and an avid yoga student. Her passion is connecting with people, especially young adults at the high school where she works. Life in 10 minutes and her Tuesday evening writing group has become her lifeline in the pandemic.

**Elizabeth Eley's** round cheeks belie her edgier personality. She enjoys the element of surprise this affords with assuming strangers. She ventured into Life in 10 to explore her truth and found a community of kindred spirits who've taught her that every type of story is worthy of writing and sharing.

**Nikiya Ellis** is a mother of three, a gardener, a farmer, beekeeper and a Reiki practitioner. As a Mother and a Birthworker, she sees the importance of giving all birthing people a fair chance at the birth they desire. Sankofa is a traditional African concept that translates to "Go back and get it," we all need to return to our roots, to reclaim the wisdom of our ancestors, to educate, inform & share knowledge to the birthing people in our diverse communities.

**Melissa Face** is the author of *I Love You More Than Coffee,* an essay collection for parents who love coffee a lot and their kids...a little more. Her essays and articles have appeared in *Richmond Family Magazine, Tidewater Family Magazine,* and *Scary Mommy.* She lives in Prince George, teaches world literature at the Appomattox Regional Governor's School for the Arts and Technology, and watches every episode of *Good Girls.* Read more at melissaface.com.

**Kali Fillhart** (she/her/hers) is a queer writer, musician, artist, and astrology nerd from Suffolk, Virginia. Kali is currently enjoying post-undergrad life by teaching herself the drums and taking care of her hairless, four-legged child Maggie. A soon-to-be Bostonian, Kali plans on pursuing her art, writing, and activism in the North East for a little while.

**Louise Gilbert Freeman,** a North Carolina native and mother of three, lives in Richmond, VA with her husband. Since she stopped teaching English at Randolph-Macon College, she has returned to her childhood love of creative writing and of oil painting.

**Hollee Freeman, PhD** is a career educator focused on equity and access. Her children's books include *Muddy Ballerinas,* centered around interracial friendships and *Beekeeping Besties: An Apiary Adventure,* based on her experience as a beekeeper.

**erin gerety** is a Richmond, Virginia based musician, artist, and radio personality. You can find their work at eringerety.com.

**David Gerson** is a writer and attorney who lives in Baltimore, MD. A collection of his work is included in Unzipped Issue 4, *Inheritance.*

**Gail Giewont** lives in Chesterfield, Virginia, with her dogs. She is a teacher in the Literary Arts department at Appomattox Regional Governor's School and has a small book of poetry, *Vulture,* available from Finishing Line Press.

**Stella Graham-Landau** is a wife poet mom artist bonus grandmother liberal feminist Richmond native crone vegan animal caregiver and takes very seriously the need to be a little bit silly at every opportunity.

**Lois Henry** is a native New Yorker and current resident of Midlothian, VA. She is a wife, mother and attorney, and writes memoir and fiction on Tuesday evenings as a member of Cindy Cunningham's Life in 10 class. Thank you to Cindy and the amazing Tuesday night group for your support and for helping me to find my voice. One day soon, we will all eat cake together.

**Donna Joyce** is a cheerleader for creativity, community and healthy personal boundaries. She believes these can lift us up, help us to feel whole, solve our problems, big and small, and change the world in beautiful and necessary ways. She is a native of New York living in Richmond, VA, with her husband of 20 years, her two children ages 16 and 11, and a bunny named Bee.

**Derek Kannemeyer's** writing has appeared in publications from *Fiction International* to *Rolling Stone*. Recent books include an international poetry chapbook contest winner; the five act "Play of Gilgamesh"; a poetry collection, "Mutt Spirituals"; and the hybrid photography/non-fiction "Unsay Their Names" (featured fall 2021 gallery show at Richmond's Black History Museum).

**Gary Kornfeld** is a writer/performer/part-time amateur photographer and he drives for a living.

**Linda Laino** is a visual artist, and writer living for almost ten years in San Miguel de Allende, Mexico. She holds an MFA from Virginia Commonwealth University, and loves finding beautiful things on the ground. Her art is here, www.lindalaino.com and some of her writing is here, wordsandpictures.lindlaino.com.

**Jer Long** is a devoted fan of Valley Haggard. Through her guidance, and the support of her amazing Thursday morning class, he tapped into the inner author he hoped to be and has recently completed his first novel, *Pollyanna Gay*, which will be available in spring 2022.

**Marie Marchand** has been published in the *Paterson Literary Review*, *Tiny Seed Literary Journal*, *High Plains Register*, *The Seattle Times*, *The Writing Cooperative*, and numerous chapbooks. Her poetry collection, *Pink Sunset Luminaries*, was published in 2018. She was recognized by the Allen Ginsberg Poetry Awards and Wyoming Writers. mishiepoet.medium.com and mishiepoet.com.

**Joan Mazza** worked as a medical microbiologist and psychotherapist, and taught workshops on dreams and nightmares. She is the author of six books, including *Dreaming Your Real Self*, and her poetry has appeared in *The MacGuffin, Prairie Schooner, Poet Lore,* and *The Nation.* She lives in rural central Virginia. www.JoanMazza.com

**Cecelia Meredith** is an author, artist & astrologer, here to celebrate the weird & wonderful of this world.

**Kristi Mullins** takes ample selfies in her hometown of Richmond, Virginia where she lives with her husband, daughter, two dogs and cat. She enjoys creating music and posting to SoundCloud, writing, painting, gardening and bragging heavily about her kid. She obtained her B.A. in English from Virginia Commonwealth University and M.B.A. from Averett University.

**Amanda Riley Smith** teaches children with autism, who she draws inspiration from daily. She loves writing, her two dogs and the Tuesday night writing group.

**Theresa Ronquillo** is a second-generation Filipina American who writes counternarratives about growing up in the Midwest. Founder of Embody Change LLC, Theresa facilitates social justice theater workshops for educators, and writing groups for the Asian American community. She lives in Richmond with her partner, teen daughter, and senior dog.

**Patricia Smith** is the author of the novel *The Year of Needy Girls,* a 2018 finalist for a Lambda Literary Award. Her nonfiction has appeared in such places as *Hippocampus, Salon, Broad Street, Feels Blind Literary, Parhelion Literary Review* and in various anthologies. She teaches at the Appomattox Regional Governor's School in Petersburg, VA and lives with her wife in Chester, VA.

**Lee Sowder's** first novel, *Family Weave,* was published in 2021. She is currently working on her second novel in Durham, NC.

**James Stoneking** is an educator at the Appomattox Regional Governor's School in Petersburg, VA as well as a life-long student of history. He has been an avid collector of antiquities and oddities for most of his life, and he enjoys inflicting his archaic knowledge on others in and outside of the classroom.

**Andrew Taylor-Troutman** is the author of five books, most recently *Hope Matters: Churchless Sermons in the Time of the Coronavirus.* He is a Presbyterian pastor and lives in Chapel Hill, North Carolina with his spouse and their three young children.

**Slats Toole** is a writer, sound designer, and musician based in Minneapolis, MN. Their poetry has been published in various magazines, and most recently the anthology "This Present Former Glory: an Anthology of Honest Spiritual Literature". Their Lenten poetry series has been compiled in the collection "Queering Lent."

**Sarah Twombly's** writing has appeared in *The New York Times, Esquire Magazine,* and *Prairie Schooner,* among others. She is a recipient of the Maine Literary Award for nonfiction, and is currently nominated for a Pushcart Prize, Best of the Net, and Best Small Fictions. She lives in the woods of Maine with her wild family and very tame dog.

**Alyssa Tyson** has been writing since she knew what words were. When she's not writing, you can find her baking way too many brownies and binge-watching the *Twilight* saga on repeat. She lives in Richmond, Virginia with the world's most spoiled cats and guinea pigs.

**Hope Whitby** is a poet, writer, and haiku aficionado living in Richmond, VA with her Chihuahua, Princess. She is the author of *Traveling the River,* a book of poems, and teaches Poetry is Possible at Life in 10 Minutes.

# Colophon

*Bare: An Unzipped Anthology* was typeset in Freight Text.

Freight Text is a serif typeface designed by Joshua Darden and published through GarageFonts in 2005. Freight is an extremely versatile superfamily with many different versions available, making it suitable for a wide range of typographic challenges. It is the type family used as part of the identity system for the National Museum of African American History and Culture in Washington D.C.

*Bare* was designed by Llewellyn Hensley & Content–Aware Graphic Design—**content-aware.design.**

# Thank you
# for supporting *Unzipped*

Our project is made possible by readers like you. We are infinitely grateful to our patrons who make it possible for us to continue publishing urgent, brave, and true stories! To learn more about supporting us through our subscription program, our online litmag, classes, and workshops, visit **lifein10minutes.com/unzipped**. We would love to write, read, and (metaphorically) unzip with you.

9 781949 246179